Aurélienne Dauguet

LIGHT-NUTRITION

MY NEW LIFE AS A BREATHARIAN

Quotation from JOHANN WOLFGANG VON GOETHE:

"In all my actions I have got used to following my heart without ever thinking either of disapproval or repercussions."

Bibliographic information from the German National Library:

The German National Library lists this publication in the German National Bibliography; detailed bibliographical data can be found on the Internet at http://dnb.dnb.de.

Production: BoD - Books on Demand, Norderstedt

The work, including its parts, is protected by copyright. Any use without the publisher's consent is inadmissible. This applies in particular to electronic or other publications, duplication, translation, distribution and other publications.

© Merano-Verlag, Kipfenberg, Deutschland

Bibliografische Information der Deutschen Nationalbibliothek:

Die Deutsche Nationalbibliothek verzeichnet diese Publikation in der Deutschen Nationalbibliografie; detaillierte bibliografische Daten sind im Internet über http://dnb.dnb.de abrufbar.

Herstellung: BoD - Books on Demand, Norderstedt

ISBN: 978-3-944700-18-2 (Paperback)

ISBN: 978-3-944700-28-1 (e-book)

Aurélienne Dauguet

LIGHT-NUTRITION

MY NEW LIFE AS A BREATHARIAN

Author: Aurélienne Dauguet

Design of the envelope, illustration: Aurélienne Dauguet

Translation: Aurélienne Dauguet

Corrections: Gert Meißner

Original title "Mein neues Leben mit der Lichtnahrung"

© Aurélienne Dauguet

This book has been designed with great care. The biographical elements reflect only the author's experiences, as well as individual reflections on pranic food. It is understood that no guarantee can be assumed for advice.

In addition, the author does not bear any responsibility for others.

Content

PREFACE 11
PART ONE: THE 21-DAY PROCESS 13
    04.04.2017 13
    06.04.2017 15
    11.04.2017 – Day 1 16
    12.04.2017 – Day 2 18
    13.04.2017 – Day 3 22
    14.02.2017 – Day 4 26
    15.04.2017 – Day 5 28
    16.04.2017 – Day 6 30
    17.04.2017 – Day 7 33
    18.04.2017 – Day 8 34
    19.04.2017 – Day 9 36
    20.04.2018 – Day 10 39
    21.04.2017 – Day 11 42
    22.04.2017 – Day 12 44
    23.04.2017 – Day 13 45
    24.04.2017 – Day 14 46
    25.04.2017 – Day 15 52
    26.04.2017 – Day 16 55
    27.04.2017 – Day 17 59
    28.04.2017 – Day 18 60
    29.04.2017 – Day 19 64
    30.04.2017 – Day 20 65

01.05.2017 – Day 21 66
PART TWO: MY GENERAL CONDITION AFTER THE INSTALLATION .. 69
   07.05.2017 69
   11.07.2017 70
   24.07.2017 71
   08.09.2017 72
   13.09.2017 76
   03.11.2017 76
   10.12.2017 77
   13.12.2017 79
   January 2018 84
   February 2018 87
   March 2018 93
   09.04.2018 96
   11.04.2018 100
PART 3: SURROUNDING THEMES 104
   1. MY MOTIVATIONS 104
   2. MY PREPARATIONS 110
   3. MY PHYSICAL METAMORPHOSIS 118
      a) During the process 118
      b) The processes within the process 122
      c) The pranic body 126
      d) The rhythms and my idiosyncrasies 127
   4. MY STATE OF MIND 132
   5. MY SPIRITUAL TRANSFORMATION 135
      a) Self-esteem and food 135

  b) My spiritual connection 137
  c) Meditation... 139
 6. SUPPORT AND ACCOMPANIEMENT 141
  a) Morphogenetic fields.. 141
  b) Guidance from various planes 143
  c) Harmonious synchronicities... 145
  d) Therapeutic help 148
  e) Support and assistance 150
 7. MY MEASUREMENTS 151
 8. REACTIONS FROM PEOPLE AROUND ME........................ 153
 9. TRANSFORMING NEGATIVE PROJECTIONS...................... 163
 10. WHAT IS LIGHT-NOURISHMENT? 168
 11. THE EFFECTS OF PRANA... 177
 12. PUBLIC RAMIFICATIONS OF PRANA NOURISHMENT......... 179
 13. CONCLUSION 181
List of my present teachings 184
THE AUTHOR... 186
Literary reference 187

PREFACE

This report about my pranic process (P.P.) is not a report of a "success trip" in the sense of a story without any difficulties: "stopped eating, didn´t lose a gram, no problems, all went well". In this exposé I wish to thoroughly describe the process itself as well as the accompanying reactions, which are not always glorious, so that people gain a more down to earth and realistic approach to breatharianism.

The change to Light nourishment exhibits many facets and concerns many personal aspects as well as various sides of daily life. In this book I am describing some of them from a modest, but adventurous perspective. I am sharing this experience with you in the hope that it is for you as enjoyable and enriching as it is for me.

Part one covers the diary of my transformation process over 21 days during which the conversion to and the installation of prana take place.

Part two is a report of my development at various random dates following the process up to a complete year ending on April 11th, 2018.

In part three I am looking at different topics which cropped up during that year in terms of observations, perceptions, explanations and conclusions gathered and drawn from my own experience.

I took the decision to become pranic in accordance with my free will, together with a deep and well reflected sense of responsibility. My reactions and my way of dealing with the process are entirely personal and individual. I emphasize that I am in no way enticing anybody to follow this path, which can only be the result of an inner response to the call of the soul.

It is important for me to go through this pranic evolution in a personal and individual manner, in alignment with my body, my soul, my spirit as well as my daily needs.

As a pioneer, I have allowed myself some neologisms. For example, I call people feeding on Light "pranics", and I use this term in a similar sense as "breatharians". The initials P.P. stands for the 21-day pranic process, which refers to the installation of the prana in the cells and in the auric field.

PART ONE: THE 21-DAY PROCESS
04.04.2017

In a week's time, I shall start the process which will enable me to live on prana. My intention is to achieve a definite change over to light nourishment until May 1st.

For me this process means a liberation and not a renunciation in the usual sense of the word. In this context renunciation is a free and well reflected decision not to introduce anything into my field that has no resonance with my personal needs and my energy. As a matter of fact, my field does not recognize any connection with solid and material foodstuff anymore, for it is getting used to a more subtle nourishment, which now resonates with the frequency of my personal present energy.

Renouncement in the way of feeling free to give up something demands on the one hand the ability of discrimination and on the other hand decisiveness coupled with a clear will and the possibility to express and manifest this conscious choice. Let us look at the ability to discriminate and we'll meet straight away with the challenge of self-observation: What makes sense to me, what is right for me? What is in accordance with me?

In order to be able to answer such questions, it is necessary to be in direct communication with the inner being through feelings, intuition and also through reflection. In other words: the prerequisites demand being in contact with one's own inner criterions and references and with the guidance of one's own soul. The latter is the highest authority of these, for it carries the remembrance of one's life mission, which follows the soul's journey. It knows exactly what is in accordance with me and my path of life and it constantly keeps in touch and communicates with my consciousness through my spiritual, mental, emotional, etheric and physical bodies.

In this context, renouncement means creating a space in order to discover further and higher levels. Higher, in the sense of more advanced on the scale of evolution, more subtle and infused with greater Light. Renouncement is also connected with awareness and freedom, allowing oneself to refuse something, in this case material and solid food. It is the conscious decision to take in nourishment of a higher qualitative value. In this approach one can hardly speak of "Ersatz", for this would imply a sense of replacement, something which is the same or has the same value. But my intention is a complete transfer to prana, to a superior alternative through which both health and vibrational level are clearly improved. This is what this report is all about.

Already as a child I had the knowledge that human beings can live without food and with much less sleep. It seemed to me that this state of being urgently had to be aimed at. For daily routine appeared to me like an eternal running around in a circle, as if humanity was condemned to be radically limited in its freedom and its development, comparable to the hamster in his cage racing around in his spinning wheel forever.

Living on solid food sets up a whole logistic string in itself, from hunting wild animals to shopping in a luxury supermarket – if we want to consider the topic of food. Our society is based on the emphasis of basic needs. By multiplying these needs and basically exploiting them its intent is on making as much profit as possible. What is the result? An inescapable roundabout of dependencies and consumption which are again sustained by having to work and earn money, precisely in order to maintain and perpetuate this compulsive habit of consuming. A continued, never ending state of slavery. Let´s make the best out of it! Until mankind arrives at another perspective and a more creative approach of dealing with needs and consumption.

The true nourishment of man, his beingness and his aliveness, are of subtle origins and are fundamentally connected to the higher dimensions.

Already as a child I had the feeling that another option was not only possible but also conceivable and realizable.

06.04.2017

Since then, I have made a few detours and committed many errors. Fasting and changing diets are not foreign to my body. They keep it young and fresh. Nevertheless it is indispensable to have a certain knowledge, to be able to observe oneself and to be caring and attentive with one's own physical body.

Two years ago, I already made an attempt to follow a P.P. Indeed, it was an enriching experience providing me with worthwhile insights, which are helpful in the present endeavor. But this time I shall do a few things differently. I shall keep to liquids and leave out the fruit juices.

About a year ago I switched over to vegan food and since then have mainly been drinking smoothies. To make them I use organic fruits and vegetables as well as wild herbs from my garden, algae, bitter spices and moringa. In the last few months I diminished the quantity and improved the quality. I already have lost some weight. I am feeling better physically and mentally. I am looking forward very much to this complete adaptation to prana which I deeply long for. But the body will have the last word: Will it agree to living on prana or not? The decision cannot come from the mind alone.

My connection to the spiritual realms is both the source of my strength and my companion and counselor. Parallel to this, it is necessary to follow and respect the reactions of the body. The psychological development will also be observed and registered.

11.04.2017 – Day 1

Full moon in the sign of Scorpio.

Today was the first day of my process changing over to pranic nourishment. First thing in the morning I had an osteopathic treatment. Immediately, I got a backache which is unusual for me. It is cold and I had to really wrap myself up warmly. The hot teas did me good and I particularly enjoyed them. I hardly felt any hunger. I am well prepared through my previous conversion to raw food and smoothies. My mind is rejoicing, and my cells are ready for the change-over. I have time for the process, so that I can do things in a quiet and posed manner. I have done some work in the garden and went shopping.

I already notice a certain sensibility when I observe people in the underground and on the bus. During the last months, sounds and smells have become unbearable for me, if they are disharmonious and unpleasant. A refinement of the senses has

already taken place and the perception of thoughts, feelings and inner moods is much more subtle. The clairvoyance and the ability to grasp the "knot" of the problem are more substantial.

The Light-food did me good and even provided me with some warmth in the body. I had to yawn a lot during meditation, which is a sign of relaxation and letting go. I felt a deep joy within, especially in the heart space. The way of taking in the Light and experiencing its effects constitute a life elixir for me. Joy is an expression of the soul. That confirms my being on the right path. The liberation from solid, physical food and the reduction of the sleep duration are some of my very old wishes, and both, the right timing and this very special opportunity, have now come to manifest this intention. I have planned this all consciously and I have prepared myself meticulously. These are all positive reasons, and I feel myself carried by a deep happiness. I am aiming at contributing to the Big Whole, to the evolution of the earth and its humanity and to the growing pranic community which lives dispersed all over the world.

Now I shall have a bath with a Swiss healing earth to alleviate my backache and to enjoy the warmth of the water. At the end of this 1st day, I am full of gratefulness.

12.04.2017 – Day 2

This day is still under the sign of Scorpio, which means depth and courage and the power for change as well as the required readiness to end existing cycles and to initiate new ones. Scorpio stands for death and rebirth in the realms of evolution through the impulse of transformation.

For my inner journey I need space and time. They are necessary to design my own spiritual landscape at my own individual pace. This enables me to recover the original source of inspiration and creativity as opposed to having outer elements managing and organizing my personal requirements and rhythms. I want to reclaim my own time. The time/space continuum within one´s own life is too often dictated from the outside and by others. These are the adversities which I resist or even completely delete out of my life, for I occasionally experience certain influences coming from outside as pure disturbances. Yes, disturbances that are hallmarked by the interruption of one´s own life flow, an estrangement from one´s own intentions and dedication. I must of course be careful not to become misanthropic, so that the nourishing and balancing retreat does not end up in an attempt to flee from the world. For all spiritual searches it is a challenge to preserve the balance between within and without. What do you possibly meet with, when you have reached your inner space? Are you coming to terms with unprocessed thoughts and feelings, daily problems, concrete organizational and material topics? Or does the perspective widen itself to a supplementary source of inspiration, introspection and recognition? If the inner space serves as an interface with ideas and energies of a higher sphere, then there is a connection, which generates something new and brings creativity and innovation into the world, at least within the personal microcosm. Everything taking place on a small scale inevitably imbues also the macrocosm and vice versa through the common quantum field.

Physicists and metaphysicians know the great paradox: there is no inner and outer on the subtle planes. Within and without are two aspects of the hologram. On one level all beings are one, on another each one is responsible for the self, knowing that every action influences the whole.

The "as well as" occupies more and more space in a world where frequency rising is taking place on the terrestrial plane. It is therefore facilitating the interaction with the higher spheres, and at the same time permeating the lower ones with their powerful, subtle vibrations in order to overflow the earth and raise its consciousness and the awareness of all beings living on it.

There are many people, also children, who have had near death experiences, who have clear and precise memories of previous incarnations and who are accustomed to the practice of meditation and other states of expanded consciousness. Whereas they would have repressed and suppressed them in the past, they now go out and share what they have lived and experienced first-hand, so that at last science takes them into consideration.

The delimitations are melting, and the various planes are interacting with each other: the monk, the sannyasin leaves the ashram and follows his path outside in the world without being led astray. Again and again he/she goes into withdrawal where he/she bathes in spirit; and so he/she manages to create and recreate a balance and develop himself/ herself in both realities.

The night was good. I found the spiritual music very nurturing. On the physiological level I had a bowel movement. Now I need to go out and get moving.

I meditate twice a day and I cultivate a quiet, peaceful and harmonious state of mind. Today I got many things done and spent quite a while in the city.

I am open but not oversensitive – a state which I occasionally experience. I can benefit from beautiful, loving surroundings, for I seem to feed on the emanation of flowers and blossoming trees. I also feel harmoniously nurtured by the sight of a young couple in love in the botanical garden. I am always receptive to beauty, colors and pleasant emotions, but today, in these wonderful surroundings, the subtle energies of the splendid vegetation are directly nurturing my aura. Today, even more intensely than yesterday, I experience a deep joy which moves me to tears. Then it dawns on me that I rarely have experienced this pure feeling lately. Contented, yes, a positive anticipation of the process, yes, but I have been missing such tears of happiness for a long time. Thank God, they are back! I could even call it blissfulness, so intense and profound is the deeply felt experience.

Physically, I notice some tensions in the lumbar region. I suppose they are signs of detoxification. Like yesterday, I yawn a lot. Another observation, which I made by listening to music, is an improvement in the hearing in my left ear, so that both ears are functioning equally well, now. But I want to test this more thoroughly later on.

I am hardly hungry. The long and precise preparation for the process has already impregnated the cells with the right intent.

In the evening I communicate with HM. He gives me good advice and confirms my need for movement. It is important to drink a lot and to move sufficiently so as to stimulate the detoxification and the elimination of stress, toxins and heavy metals out of the muscles and the joints. I am acquainted with such measures through my work as a nurse in the Bircher-Benner clinic. This was a naturopathic clinic, was established by Dr. Bircher-Benner in the 1930's and represented one of the "regulation therapies" mainly based on dietary components, especially the well-known Bircher Müesli. Other factors, such as movement, fresh air and keeping up with natural rhythms also played an important part in this concept.

But now I feel tired and I go to bed early.

13.04.2017 – Day 3

During the night I pass water several times. But it is a long and deep sleep during which I am woken up once by a hunger feeling. I soothe it with a few sips of water. Today, I was again very active which is enjoyable, but I also need rest and peace.

I have to strengthen my grounding and my vitality to prevent me from leaving my body time and time again.

I have a slightly accelerated heart-rhythm which I remember from the last process. When I generally harmonize my state, my heart benefits from it and it quiets down. I am thirsty and drink a lot which I find pleasurable. I really look forward to a cup of herbal tea. I like drinking warm or hot beverages, because it is cold. The low temperature is difficult to put up with, and I have to ensure that I dress warmly.

My tongue is slightly coated, the light headache from yesterday evening has gone. Through physical activity and sufficient liquids, I easily manage to get rid of detoxification pains in the muscles.

I like and appreciate myself more than usual. I feel confident and everything seems easy.

Not only do I need to thoroughly purify myself, but I want to put a new order to my apartment. I am discovering a new connection to order, not only in the usual sense, but in the awareness of a higher or even the highest order within which everything is as it should be, because everything occupies the space which it is intended to occupy.

Occasionally, images and sense-felt emotions of mistreatments in other incarnations are cropping up. Then they disappear, only to reappear a short time later in my mind. They are not tormenting me, but they are still present. The actual state I am in reminds me of the time when I stopped smoking. Actually, the P.P. is also about getting rid of addictions.

In the morning I was busy with washing and tidying up. Now I want to clean my ears, my nose, my tongue and my bowels. As a nurse with knowledge and experience in the naturopathic domain as well as numerous trainings in the spiritual field, I have great resources at my disposal, in both the subtle and the physical areas. In this way I can take the various aspects into account, observing them individually as well as in their interaction, and treat them accordingly. A precise self-observation is extremely important, in order to grasp exactly the state in which I find myself, to make out what the needs are and to fulfill and harmonize them, and finally draw the right conclusions.

I am glad I have learnt to give an enema. It is a simple procedure, which should be done very carefully, for there are a couple of important points which have to be taken into account for a safe procedure. Everybody should know of this cleansing method, for it relieves a lot of ailments: from headache to bad skin as well as colds; and it is generally a good remedy against feeling unwell. Enemas can be applied as a self-help measure. But who wants to deal with excrements in our clean society?

Who does not rather prefer to swallow a couple of tablets and to go through some expensive tests to find out where the next illness is coming from? This is no prophylaxis but rather an expectation that the body is made to break down. This is not my reality!

As I have already mentioned, observation is of the utmost importance. I regularly watch my urine and I can clearly assess that the elimination is on the way. I drink as much as is required so as to reach a clear yellow to colorless urine. Also, in normal daily life it makes sense to adjust the amount of fluids according to the personal needs instead of systematically drinking 2 or 3 liters a day, as is generally recommended. Each person is an individual being and each one reacts differently in accordance to temperature, physical efforts, food intake etc. depending upon his/her size and constitution as well as many other factors and functions. While monitoring the color of the urine one can find out what is right for oneself by adjusting the right amount of fluids in an individual manner at any given time. Some people tend to drink too much, so that they get rid of the good things their body should retain such as trace elements, minerals etc. Then these have to be replenished with artificial alternatives. Good for the pharmaceutical industry. Why not rather follow the signs of the body? Your body is constantly talking to you! Pure filtered water is better than any other liquid. But this is a topic of its own.

In the afternoon I feel the fatigue and need a rest. I listen to spiritual music which is nurturing me on all levels.

Today I dedicated a bunch of flowers in light green, magenta and pink colors to my P.P. I am interpreting the colors in the following manner: pale green for a new beginning in the Light and the Truth. This is the path without compromise of Hilarion, the strict teacher, whose reward is so generous, if the student has understood the lesson. Astrologically, he is under the influence of Saturn, who reminds us of the path chosen by the soul. Magenta stands for the expression of divine love and divine healing. In this color the ideal, the highest conception and representation of the present incarnation yearns for the path that is in accordance with the essence, journeying between Alpha and Omega. Pink is the all-embracing love, the love of all and everything that is. I consider each single flower individually and place it in a particular order so as to represent various levels of consciousness. For this process is mainly a matter of awareness and consciousness within the different realms, but it is also following a specific succession of steps from one layer to the other. The bunch is tall, but also wide. The magenta anemones form a spiral yearning upwards and are surrounded by a green and pale-green background. Right at the top the pale pink flowers throne victoriously. Two pale-green carnations with very light pink lines on their petals rise up high in front and form a triangle in combination with a single one at the opening of the vase. As it where they symbolize the connection between my guidance and myself. As I am able to communicate with the vegetal world, I receive the impression that the two white ranunculi with a pale violet edge are feeling too tight there and would prefer to be in a small vase on their own. This bunch of flowers is a symbol for my process precisely through the choice of colors and forms as well as through the neat order of each of its blossoms. I wish to add one more thing: Carnations possess a high vibration and open up the connection to and the communication with spirit.

Early in the evening I feel tired and soon go to bed.

14.02.2017 – Day 4

It was a rather long but unquiet night, for I was woken up by heart palpitations. I became acquainted with them during the last process and from situations which occasionally torment and by which I am revolted because of their injustice or appalling character, situations like war, prostitution or poverty, situations which are intentionally instigated. The essential oil of lavender helps me to go back to sleep quickly.

As I get up in the morning, it is obvious that my blood circulation is affected and that my blood pressure is really low, so that I can hardly get up. As I try to make coffee, I have an outburst of perspiration and all my strength leaves me. I lie down on the floor and put my legs up. It is helpful and I manage to get to the cupboard, take a pinch of salt and make a cup of coffee.

As soon as I have recovered, I feel like going to the park. Even if I am a little weak at the beginning the movement is stimulating and I regain my strength! I discover a swan that has built its nest near to the lakeside. I am quite impressed by it, for it is the first time I see a swan brooding. I shall often visit it, in a tactful manner, of course. On the roadside I notice lily of the valley, of which I would like to pick a few stems when it is blossoming.

As I come back home, I carry out the meditation which is accompanies my transformation and provides me with prana. The hot herbal teas do me good and give me the warmth that I lack. It is Easter and it is still cold. I probably have lost weight, and that will account for the sensitivity to the cold.

The cat that is living in the area and is being fed by various neighbors started visiting me lately. She is communicating telepathically, but her behaviour and her hissing are also very clear. I immediately see in her aura, that she is ill and weak. I have been treating her for the last week. At the beginning she was rather distant, but now she is sleeping on my lap on the patio. We both enjoy this, but as I get cold and want to go inside and turn up the heating, I have to disturb her sleep. She reacts very angrily and miaows loudly. I am freezing!

My inspiration guides me to use a stick of antimonite to clear my aura and stabilize my accelerated pulse. This is helpful. The stone also grounds me. Then I have the idea of breathing down into my belly. Little by little my state improves. It is all helping slightly but at 5.30 pm my heartbeat is still very fast making me feel slightly dizzy. So I treat myself with the violet color and transfer a Bach remedy energetically into my aura.

The tachycardia is still there. I take more salt and this time use the color black, after which I immediately feel an improvement. The beating of my heart becomes quieter. I do my physical exercises and cleanse my nose, my bowels and my tongue.

I feel an urge to put the objects around me all in order. This is astonishing, for on the whole I am not disorderly. But there are always small and new improvements to make. This tendency started right at the beginning of the process. Honestly, I am glad to have time to purify the whole flat with effective microorganisms and make everything look really bright.

The unpleasant thoughts reminding me of previous lives have ceased. I am not hungry, and I have no interest in food either.

This evening, I am staying up longer and I feel the fatigue much later than the three previous days. The palpitations are quieter.

I am feeling very well. This pleases me greatly, compared to how I felt first thing in the morning.

15.04.2017 – Day 5

Today the tachycardia is present all day but not as intensively as yesterday. The music "The voice of the heart" and the use of the antimonite do me good. I also program the three levels of the heart: physical, emotional and spiritual.

I am feeling the cold much more than usual and I need warm clothing, heating and a hot water bottle. It is indeed really cold!

I have a little backache, which I can't manage to relieve, neither with the comfrey ointment nor with the arnica oil. Before I go to bed, I shall have a bath with a special healing earth. While reading I notice a slight worsening in my eyesight, which I assume to be part of the detox symptoms.

In the afternoon I feel a slight fatigue, which wanes after a little nap. Afterwards I am even more active in the cellar and bring up all the literature which I have collected about pranic nourishment. Then I go to the botanical garden. Music, flowers and plants have a nurturing effect upon me and make me happy.

I charge water with the following intent: "Definitive conversion to breatharian nourishment on all levels: physical, emotional, mental, mind and spirit in a gentle and safe manner until May 1st. Thank you."

This phase, which is considered the installation of the Light within the prana body, can also be viewed from another perspective. The Light is permeating All That Is, always and everywhere. We are bathing in it and are constantly part of it. Actually, it is all about reactivating a function deep down within the cells which is presently closed down. It has nothing to do with bringing something new or foreign into being. This is, at least, how I conceive it.

From tomorrow onwards I shall program my weight so that I do not lose too much, for I do not have much reserve.

I feel guided and protected and I am happy and grateful for going through this process.

16.04.2017 – Day 6

Strong palpitations woke me up during the night. And when I get up, the tachycardia intensifies itself even more. I take my needs into account and attend to them. I treat myself energetically and radionically. I can comprehend the development and know that everything is happening in a safe realm.

I am losing weight, as is often the case at the beginning. I notice a bruise at a place which is always a little sensitive and painful, although I have no visible wound there; nevertheless, a small trauma in the cell memory. This is part of the processes of the first week: physical information in the body tissues makes itself noticeable, in order to be resolved or cancelled.

The space around me is bright, even the cellar where I collect the washing appears to be illuminated. My perception is cleansed and rearranged by prana. In the meantime, I have a lot of energy and a great need for movement. It is raining outside. However, I am looking forward to a nice and rapid walk.

My sister calls me just as I am getting dressed to go out. Three weeks ago, we had an intensive conversation and we cleared some of our differences and reached a satisfying reconciliation. Since then a trustful relationship is growing between us. This makes me happier and lighter. After a while I nearly have to interrupt her word flow, for we have now been speaking for a long time and I cannot hold back my urge to go out anymore. I need to spend my energy on a long big walk.

As I have mentioned, I have a lot of strength even an overload which I want to get rid of. I receive a hint from my guidance. I have to get some insights which will then bring me a deep peace. I obtain something like an overview of the last few days, especially about the ill treatments in previous incarnations. The cellular memory of these tortures expresses itself through the hyperactivity of my heart-muscle. Indeed, it is part of the process to have experiences surfacing into awareness, to be worked on and eliminated eventually. As a matter of fact, it is a bit too early, for the first week rather deals with physical reactions. However, the correlations are clear to me. And even more interesting connections are surfacing: The second trauma that is influencing the heart palpitations has to do with prenatal imprints. I am aware of the atmosphere surrounding the time of my birth and the events that were taking place between my parents and how they left their imprint in my cells. Indeed, I can confirm the present recognitions through the knowledge I gained in regressions, through what my mother told me and also through the insights I got during therapeutic sessions. Moreover, I learn that my soul has chosen these parents in order to achieve healing in depth as well as spiritual transformation, which is, among other things, unfolding now.

The tachycardia is diminishing but still not completely gone. I am going back home – and guess who is waiting for me in the garden? The three-colored cat who I have named Mimin in the meantime. For the first time she walks into my flat, where it is warm, and even accepts my invitation to sit on my lap. My treatment relieves her pain, and her aura expands. She is enjoying it and purrs as she has never done before. At the beginning of our acquaintance she was very miserly with purring. I had even named her "the cat that doesn`t purr". She is nevertheless very thoughtful while sitting on my lap and observes the apartment from this advantageous position. After 20 minutes she goes to the door and tries to open it with her paw. And Good-Bye!

I am exhausted from this inner work and my overactive heart. I make myself comfortable on the bean bag and cover myself so that I am warm and protected. There is still a fact to be revealed so as to understand the cause and origin of the palpitations. To connect with it I should deepen my state of consciousness. This is why I go into an alpha-state and a focused meditation.

Otherwise the day is peaceful. I take a lot of liquids; I have no sensation of hunger and gradually my heart-rhythm becomes quieter. I test whether there are any energetic needs that I should attend to.

During the process I only work with a few clients. I mainly do distance work giving feedback on the phone. Right now, a very satisfied mother just called. Her son is reacting positively to my work.

17.04.2017 – Day 7

My sleep was shorter and regenerating: 6 hours.

I feel light and fit. The heart situation is not quite settled, yet the prana has cleared and cleansed the bowels.

I am working on my emotional body with radionics so as to clear it of its slags. For the first time in the last two days I am going to town and I am surprised how well I feel there, as usual, so to speak. During the first days I wanted to take it easy, because my grounding was not so stable, and I consequently tended to be rather sensitive. So I avoided the city atmosphere. But now I feel stronger.

I am very busy at home and complete tasks which were left undone in my day to day life. I am particularly satisfied tidying up and sorting out my personal working notes and patterns which serve as a basis for my research. Somebody who is not "initiated" in my notices would hardly be able to decipher them, for they look particular, indeed. They have been gathered over years of studying in different languages and through a lot of practice, and they do look rather esoteric. But they enable me to rapidly detect disharmonies in the subtle bodies and to work out the optimal solutions to make them recover their balance. On the whole my mood is reflective and peaceful. I am very happy being involved in this process. It is an adventure and it makes me go beyond my limits to reach a higher spiritual plane and try out another way of life. The old patterns do not function anymore, neither on a personal nor on a societal level.

18.04.2017 – Day 8

The day starts with health topics. It snowed during the night, and I always feel the effect of snow very distinctly. As soon as I get up, I notice that my blood pressure is very low. I find it hard to stand up. I manage to get to the kitchen and drink yogi tea to activate the yang and use vetiver oil to ground and strengthen myself. I remember my very etheric phase when I deeply hated the smell of vetiver. This morning it not only smells interesting, but it revives me. A fascinating discovery. Gradually I feel better, but it needs time till I can stand and walk around.

At last my blood circulation is stable and I am able to air and fumigate the rooms. Here is Mimin in my ground floor apartment. Most of the time she comes in unseen and without a sound, and I let out a little cry of surprise when I suddenly realize her presence. But she now knows me inside out and doesn´t even mind. Her visit is very short because neighbors are feeding her again, and the things I bought for her just stand around untouched. I keep on treating her radionically and her state is definitely improving. In the afternoon the snow is melting, and the sun is shining. So goodbye, I have to get out and move. This is also benefiting the blood circulation.

The fast walk definitely strengthens me. I particularly feel the cold during the process. The digestive process normally generates a lot of energy and warmth as I used to experience when I was eating late in the evening. The superfluous heat was so unpleasant that it kept me awake. I decided to completely ban late meals from my list of habits. My organism is not yet stabilized on prana and the cold is a challenge. The temperature in the apartment is higher than usual, even in the middle of winter.

Several things happened on the spiritual level. A wolf and a spider appear to me in a hypnagogic state. The wolf walks from right to left in a rather slow, steady pace without paying attention to me. Afterwards a very beautiful spider with psychedelic colors appears, to which I immediately feel a strong connection. Both of them are my totem animals. Their behavior confirms that my instincts agree with the P.P, as they both behave peacefully. I may ask them for their help and support. The wolf represents freedom, family and clan. The spider weaves the individual and collective events of the world. It is an extremely important animal for me, for she is weaving my reality. Numerologically, the spider corresponds to the number 8. She is a symbol of eternity and immortality. I always have had an affinity for spiders, and I used to keep different sorts in a terrarium. They are the only animals which you can find absolutely everywhere, in the water, down in obscure caves, up in the stratosphere. There are a lot of different species, some of which are still not listed. They are very adaptable. For example, the ones dwelling in the dark are blind. I was so fascinated by them that I even became a member of the Royal Society of Arachnology. I did not make any scientific contribution, but I was particularly interested to hear of other people sharing this interest and that they even have founded an association. At home, in the autumn and in the winter, when the spiders occupy the buildings, I enjoy their presence, for they are said to bring about luck and choose harmonious houses. I like to observe how they react to noise and slight changes in the surroundings in a very sensitive manner. But by the time of spring cleaning they get thrown out of the flat, unless they have not yet gone back to mother-nature on their own.

I have noticed that my work with radionics has improved and intensified itself. My perception of the aura has become more thorough and deeper.

19.04.2017 – Day 9

This morning my state is much better, but my usual strength is somehow lacking. My heart beats are still too fast, even if not quite as rapid as they have been before. I am not feeling so cold today. Actually, the P.P. is usually recommended during the warm season, because the weight loss makes one prone to the cold. I really did not expect it to snow at Easter.

Something quite unusual is taking place now: I have been drinking coffee in the morning for decades and in the last couple of years, mainly wild coffee from Ethiopia. It is mild and tasty. But this morning I do not feel like it. My body does not need it, does not want it. The withdrawal from coffee can be very unpleasant and even cause strong headaches. In the clinic Bircher-Benner I looked after a lot of patients exhibiting withdrawal symptoms from caffeine. They suffered a lot not only hours, but sometimes even days. I conclude that coffee is a drug when taken in large and regular amounts. Besides, caffeine is an alcaloid. So I am expecting to get a headache on this occasion. But on the contrary, my condition is getting better and better. I am not only free of pain, but I am recovering my strength, and towards the end of the day I am feeling really well.

In the afternoon I spend several hours in the city. I meet a friend who asks me how I spent Easter. I have shared news of the P.P. with few persons only and I certainly shall not mention it without good reasons. I usually answer questions in an honest manner without inventing stories for the sake of meeting people's expectations. The P.P. is one of the most important decisions of my life and I have been busy with it for years preparing myself, especially in the last two years I was pursuing these preparations with a decisive power and an intense longing. I am thoroughly convinced it is the right thing for me now. This is why I give Brigit a simple, short and truthful answer. At first, she does not understand what I am trying to explain to her. As a matter of fact it has nothing to do with understanding and intelligence but with a limited range in one's life-concepts.

As I give her further explanations, she cannot take in anymore and goes over to "giving advice".

Today my thoughts are with my family, more precisely with my ancestries. I was lucky enough to both know my grandparents as well as my great-grandparents. My education let me enjoy a lot of freedom and I was often asked what I wanted to do, which language I wanted to learn, whether I wanted to study at university. Nevertheless, at the age of 18, after my A levels, as I announced that I wanted to go out into the big wide world namely to England, my wish was fulfilled. I now recognize how much my family has given to me. I feel deeply moved and regret having sometimes judged them so harshly. There was a period when I mainly focused on family obstacles. This perspective may have had to do with the insights I gained through the therapeutic work I was doing. Maybe it correlates with a kind of stubbornness on my part. Since my youngest years, I remember, that I took each discouragement or interdiction as if it was just the right thing to aim at – whether it took two days or 20 years. Sayings like:" You can´t do that, it´s not possible, you won´t make it!" are just the greatest impulses one can give me to get my determination going and tackle things that interest me. In particular I remember my great-grandmother uttering such statements. But this does not apply to my parents, who both gave me so much, precisely through their contrasting characters. From my mother I inherited the intuition, the feeling side, the capacity to love, compassion, but also the love of nature, pantheism. My father was autodidactic and incredibly versatile, an intellectual and an artist, as well as politically active until his later years, when he got interested in shamanism. The fact that my family was lacking interest in spirituality was for a long time a source of frustration to me. Nevertheless, they had many other valuable approaches to many different things! The women were rather pragmatic, while the men tended to be pioneers. They all belong to the stream of renewal that enhances evolution. Now and especially today, I am grateful I chose these parents and that I was born into this family. I thank them all from the bottom of my heart. I am also grateful that they do not oppose my P.P. which could be an issue even with them now being disincarnated beings. On the contrary, I see them smiling and agreeing. They even rejoice with me, thanks to their tolerance and because they respect my decision as well.

20.04.2018 – Day 10

Today there is a definite change: My strength is coming back, and the heart palpitations are quieter. The intestines have emptied themselves, which I did not expect any more on the 10th day. The metabolism goes on functioning, so there is still rubbish to get rid of.

I am able to do a lot of things today with a clear head.

In the last few days I was confronted with fears caused by the tachycardia. It is interesting to know that disturbances of the heart rhythm affecting all age groups are the main reason for hospitalization. Erratic heart rhythms are frightening, because they deprive the suffering person of air and are connected with the fear of dying. This organ stores emotional wounds and some of the following patterns: yearning to be loved, not accepting oneself, not perceiving the divine within, not wanting to feel, shutting up through the fear of getting hurt – all of which do not allow the expression of the heart either.

The heart is the connecting organ to other beings and with All That Is and everything alive. The heart is the reservoir of emotions, feelings and sensations as well as of emotional wisdom.

Where are intuition, sympathy, compassion, consideration, openness, freedom in a heart that is encapsulated? In such a heart everything is frozen and solidified.

The heart is directly connected to the nervous system, for it naturally beats through the impulses which are sent from the nerves. An overloaded nervous system will violently discharge its overflow of electrical impulses – in this case into the heart muscle. Shocks and emotions are powerful forces which can make you sick if they are suppressed or repressed. If they come out vehemently, they immediately are kept under medical control instead of being transformed and eliminated in a gentle and safe way with the help of aromatherapy, Schüssler salts, energetic remedies and psychotherapy, for example. That kind of medical treatment is a guaranteed path to developing a heart disease. The main lesson lies in learning to cultivate relaxation, inner peace and the ability to gain a healthy distance. And last but not least, introspection plays an important role without which one would tend to repeat the same behavior over and over again.

My heart has revealed a lot about myself to me, about my mother who suffered from emphysema and about this society in which heart qualities are neglected. Together with the clearing which is taking place during the P.P. a lot of patterns belonging to one's own family as well as to the whole of humanity are being lived through and overcome. It would not make sense to run to the emergency station! In such a case one should rather put an end to the process.

It is my task to bring all levels in alignment with each other. The daily meditation to charge myself with prana or Light – and I prefer to call it Light – is getting more and more nurturing and its vibration increasingly radiating. Here I would like to emphasize the difference between anorexia and the P.P.: anorexia is a fight with the ego and implies self-destructive aspects. Feeding on light establishes a connection to the cosmic Light. The physical body has to be healthy. A thorough preparation is indispensable, a spiritual orientation important and a thorough cleansing and clearing of one's own problems are prerequisites. An excellent relationship to the Higher Instance is the fundamental rule. It is no game for cowards or self-proclaimed esoteric freaks, and it is not to be confused with weight-reducing diets.

21.04.2017 – Day 11

The first half of the day is pure chaos. During the second part everything gets solved and sorted out.

Right from the beginning the excitement about my heart starts again. It performs unreasonably big jumps in my thoracic cage which in turn makes me even more nervous.

I wake up from a rather tense dream with a funny note. It takes place at a time when I was still married. I am sitting in a very elegant restaurant with my ex-husband. I am served an exquisite dish. The decoration consists of a branch of blossoming and delightfully smelling lilac. I am astonished, although I find the idea original but a little ridiculous. I am wondering: Is lilac edible? Shall I make a compliment? The grotesque situation is getting more and more embarrassing and I am feeling out of place. Then a noise from outside wakes me up!

Then I go to town to collect something which is not available anymore. At the moment I tend to get particularly upset over little things. But something worse is waiting for me at home. All kinds of catastrophes related to acquaintances and friends. The whole thing gets topped by a client whom I have been following up for the last three weeks and who has just been hospitalized with acute heart problems supposedly coupled with an autoimmune illness, the doctors say.

How can that be?

My heart nearly bursts out of my thoracic cage.

I wonder whether I should faint or start relaxing. I decide to drink a cup of tea and to ask for celestial help. Then I deal with one case after the other. Little by little the various situations are clearing up.

I look upon this constellation as at a mirror of some inner confusion which I occasionally get drawn into. Today I got them served up in an exemplary manner – without any lilac as decoration.

Lesson 1: Gain more inner? distance from little unpleasant things in your life, which get blown up into over dimensional problems. This is called the syndrome of importance. Today I have the possibility to observe my reaction patterns and to straighten up some distorted reality manifestations.

Lesson 2: It is appreciable that doctors envisage the heaviest alternatives in the diagnostic processes so that all eventualities are covered, and nothing gets left out or overlooked. However, they should keep their assumptions to themselves, until the condition has been definitely diagnosed instead of immediately overwhelming patients with supplementary shocks by mentioning the worst diagnosis. This comment also applies to the nursing and all other staff members dealing with examinations and tests. Are they not aware of the damages that they are causing by this thoughtlessness? A little consideration is urgently needed there.

I test straightaway how serious the state of my client really is. Of course, there are clear diversions from the norm, but the danger is not that high. As I share the results of my measurements with her, she is able to recover from the shock and get confident again.

And I, too, find peace and quietness again and sit outside in the sun.

The big weight loss has stabilized itself after the programming of the first week. My skin is not hanging as one could expect after a diet, and that is precisely the difference prana nutrition makes. For please do not forget: Losing weight is not my purpose; my intent is to thoroughly purify all levels with the help of the Light and install prana in order to achieve a complete conversion to a pranic way of life. Now I have reached the middle of the process. My heart is beating peacefully and regularly. And tomorrow is a new day.

22.04.2017 – Day 12

Today all upsets find a solution. Even my blood circulation regains its regular rhythm. A deep relaxation is installing itself in my organism and I start harvesting the first crop of the transformation. I am very happy to be able to resume the fitness exercises which I stopped because of the tachycardia. They are invigorating and activate the inner warmth which I am lacking so much at the moment due to loss of weight.

I notice that I only have lost the superfluous weight and that I am recovering the slender body of my youth. Through this change I have regained my gracility and the tightness of the tissues. Nothing is hanging down or looking sick. The skin of my face has become cleaner and a couple of skin alterations which I have had for years have now disappeared. Physical movement is basic and even indispensable. It is doing me a lot of good. Besides the five Tibetans I do ten somersaults, one after another, so as to massage my spine and catch up upon the inactivity of the last few days. The body is our animal aspect. It must be taken into account and adequately cared for. This is indeed a very personal matter that may vary from time to time. The more satisfied the body is, the quieter it keeps and the better it serves us.

This peacefulness of the body is a favorable basis to dedicate oneself to spirituality.

The light meditation nurtures me on all levels, and little by little the change-over to prana is taking place. As soon as the whole being agrees to it in all its dimensions, the process unfolds in a gentle and elegant manner.

23.04.2017 – Day 13

A very active day is starting after a short but deep sleep.

Unfortunately, vague fears crop up, accompanied by heart palpitations. I recognize some of them as part of my uncertainties and fears. Others, however, are not my own but rather belong to the general fears that humanity has gathered over the eons – not only fears of failing, of feeling inadequate or the fear of the unknown, but also the worries of daily life. Actually, these are the doubts and negative projections which many people carry around with them. I need a little while until I can shake them off and dissolve them.

The immigrants are a present topic today: first of all, with a film by the Finnish director Aki Kaurismäki and the wonderful first meeting of all voluntary helpers of immigrants at Marienplatz. Even Konstantin Wecker is there and of course he cannot just leave it at a simple speech. And much to the joy of everyone present on this large square he sings one of his songs.

Today was a nice day. I feel very grateful for it.

24.04.2017 – Day 14

Five hours sleep, weight 50,60 kg. A great deal of energy available.

The pranic state gets installed during this last week of the PP. Its three criterions are: sleep reduction, weight stabilization and a good energy level. If they are not fulfilled, the process should not be continued after the 21 days, for it shows that the organism has not completely accepted the transformation.

Today I had an in-depth session with a client who is suffering from overweight. But she does not see it that way. She repeatedly claims that her medical results are normal, but at the same time complains about her articulations, her menopause, her family, God and everybody else. All kinds of reasons are being considered except the obvious. Just as the politicians do. Could any of these health experts who she regularly consults prescribe her a fasting cure to relieve her articulations and her metabolism? No. Overweight is normal. To hate your body because it has become formless and painful is normal. To feel bad during menopause is normal. There are tablets against this. And the results are normal. Everything is normal. It is also normal not to feel well and still to accept it. How can you feel well in a body that is overworked by too much food of a lesser quality and at the same time fighting off toxins? How can the brain receive clear thoughts, if the synapses are blocked or simply missing, and how can sufficient good mood hormones (serotonin and dopamine) be produced by a sluggish endocrine system? How can feelings of self-acceptance, self-worth, inner safety and self-assurance unfold within such a constellation? Self-pity and depression set in. And what do we do now?

We have tablets for you. Tablets which will make you feel better. With which you will put on even more weight, with which you will be even more separated from your feelings (which makes everything seem more bearable), and on which you will develop a dependency. This is very profitable for us. It makes sense all the way. Food industry and pharmaceutical industry work hand in hand. And you are in a vicious circle, you have no choice. Or this is what you believe, but it is not true. It is the illusion of powerlessness.

Dear client, actually it is the call to empowerment. Take your life in your own hands! Decide for yourself, maybe for the first time in your life. Jump out of your program and really do something for your body and for your right of self-determination instead of obeying foreign concepts and fulfilling them thoughtlessly!

Yes, I know, the mountain seems impossible to climb. The circumstances are so unbearable that you do not know where to start. And believe me, I have often been standing in front of such obstacles. Believe me, you have my entire compassion!

But precisely when everything looks denuded of meaning and as if you have reached a dead end, it is a call to start changing things. It is a call to transformation, to discover new resources together with an iron determination. Precisely under these circumstances it is worth doing an assessment, in order to make a new start and to ask for help (a difficult task for proud little ego). Yes, maybe also to practice humility (This is not servility, but it is similar to asking for guidance in a foreign city). Have the courage to ask a question, and you will get an answer! No question, no chance to get an answer! Ask the right people for help, your Higher Self, the Light Worlds, the Divine or who and whatever is trustworthy for you. And you will receive help. Always. Of course, you have to be able to recognize it. Maybe it is not always obvious. On the opposite/On the other hand, the tablet looks like an easy alternative. You swallow something that seems to solve all your problems. There will be a few other traps on the path to your own self. This little game is here to sharpen your ability of discrimination.

But you do possess the qualities of decisiveness and self-determination. So you will not swallow the tablet of disempowerment, but you will go on looking and asking, and you will be changing.

As promised, the answer always comes. Now your sense of response-ability is entering into the game. So you give your own answer to the question. Then I will make a suggestion to you, a soft and gentle possibility to improve your well-being and reduce your weight. Of course, the implementation lies entirely in your own hands, depending on your endurance and your determination. But your answer to this solution is full of doubts: Does it taste good? My answer is: no, not as good as your plate of sausages, which you eat every evening for supper. That is so, indeed.

We have many choices, but only if we have the courage and the drive to use them for our self-determination can we improve the situation. Otherwise you fall into the next trap: comfort, lethargy, fullness, lying around on the sofa ... All this leads straight to disempowerment. Indeed, it is so much easier to be idle than to gather your strength and to make the next effort.

Take on the challenge! Wake up! Gather your last strengths, which are definitely not the last ones! On the contrary, they are the ones that show you the way to your true resources and open up unexpected horizons, if you are daring enough to enter on the new path in front of you.

A plate of sausages or prana? That is the question! I take the second one, please! It tastes much better to me and fulfills me on all levels. Thank you!

No, prana is not suitable for everybody. There is no general nutritional diet that is valid for everybody. None, not even Light, although we naturally all take in some of it on a daily basis. The Light is the basic fundament of life, our livelihood, and it actually and precisely determinates to which degree we are alive. But each of us must make a choice. Between light nutrition and a plate of sausages there are quite a few other possibilities, are there not? Especially in Europe, where we are so spoilt, we should appreciate this variety with each bite. We are exploiting the whole world, the animals and the earth in order to produce this limitless abundance. Consumption disgusts me, because it is unethical, unfair, compulsive and enslaving. Even the business with organic products follows these rules. And I am not excluding myself. I have also known the tendency to eat too much, because I cannot stop until I feel bad, either out of frustration or habit. Greed. The fear not to get enough. It is the first time that this humanity (There were other humanities before.) has such an abundance of merchandise at its disposal. Generally, people suffered from famines, lack and privation at all times, recurrently and for various reasons. Today you can buy everything, everywhere, independent from any season, whatever and whenever you want. If we do not question this senseless consumption, the danger arises that you will be degraded from king to slave. The questions to ask sound like this: Why does such a small proportion of human beings benefit from such an overflow, while the majority can hardly live decently, although so much is being produced? How much of that abundance is really nurturing, how much of it can the cell really make use of? How much of it is rubbish, how much toxins, how much pesticides, antibiotics etc? How much of it makes us sick, fat, lethargic in spirit and body? Put these questions, not only to others but first of all to yourself. Analyze and scrutinize and dissect the answers, take decisions and go your own way.

I choose the path of the light warrior in the manner of Pallas Athena, the path of the pioneer, the path of my soul, my Higher Instance.

Today is a wonderful day. The sun is shining – for the first time since the beginning of the process. I am feeling well, and light and I have a lot of strength. Through the activity my heart rhythm is recovering and finding a balanced rhythm.

Just to give a little idea of how fit my body is I mention the physical activities I do on a daily basis: the 5 Tibetans 21 times each, 10 somersaults, I walk many kilometers on end through the park or along the river barefoot and I work in the garden. In the evening I go to town.

25.04.2017 – Day 15

Six hours sleep is enough for plenty of energy.

The sleep is deeper and its duration shorter. The inner peace and the regeneration are more intensive. I wake up with the lightness and freshness of a child and I am full of joy to get up at 4 am driven by youthful curiosity. What is going to happen today? How does my body react? My mind? My soul? I notice that I move in a gentler and more caring manner, that I consider other people with more empathy and admire and appreciate the world around me even more. Not that I completely lacked these qualities before, but I take time to experience the P.P. in a thoroughly conscious way and I am more considerate with myself. I am so well prepared through my spiritual and naturopathic experiences and experiments as well as my two years of preparation, that I can follow my observations on many different levels and practically apply whatever may be necessary. Concretely, that means that I deal with all my reactions equally seriously, not only with the spiritual aspect and not only with what is working out and glorious. I also communicate with my body, my emotions etc. and ask them: Dear body, how are you feeling today? What do you need and why?

Well, sometimes I get the answer even before I have asked the question and know: Oh dear, it definitely feels uncomfortable there! I shall have to attend to it!

I am well-grounded and realistic, even if I used to tend to fly off to and hover in the highest spheres when I was young – until I did lose the ground under my feet. My profession as a nurse has brought me in touch with the human, practical and pragmatic side of life. Moreover, my own body taught me a couple of lessons through sickness and even serious health problems. It has a very clear language: I do not like this – and the message is expressed through pain or discomfort. My body demands that I lend all my attention to it. I cannot ignore it, but I should not overreact to its partly very dramatic modes of expression.

The physical body with its relatively slow rhythm has something to communicate to the mind. It is an earthly lesson and that is why it appears to be so slow compared to thoughts or spiritual levels. The physical, material body is ruled by the saturnian principle, the strict teacher who generously rewards his student when he/she has understood the lesson. He is the teacher that shows how humans, as spiritual beings, can develop on the manifestation level precisely through what seems to be the limitations of the material world such as possessing a body or experiencing earth bound laws like gravity, for example. He provides us with challenges, which are invitations to listen within, to study, discover and finally to understand. Until we are ready for the next level.

Well, my dear body, what is my overactive heart telling me? I have looked at some negative attitudes of mine, done heart meditations, asked for forgiveness, I have done relaxation and breathing exercises. I know quite a few methods, believe me. The best and the most effective ones. And they do bring some relief. And my heart recovers its peaceful rhythm from time to time. But then it starts beating again like crazy. So I go on treating body and mind, even if I do not entirely grasp the logic of its palpitations. A little humility is always good for the intellect, I tell myself. The day is cold and rainy, which I find difficult to bear with. I successfully get things done which needed sorting out for a long time. Now everything is up to date: cleaning, clearing, bringing a new order in all domains. Late that afternoon, I have an appointment with the osteopath. As she tests me kinesiologically, she confirms that I have more energy than usually (not that I would be devoid of strength otherwise). As usual, she works on the whole body. Among other things she massages my gallbladder with one finger for about 45 seconds. The little organ bubbles, and I immediately understand: there is still something in it, namely glutinous secretion. This blocked secretion has to be eliminated. At the end of the treatment the osteopath recommends me to consult my GP, if the heart problems should go on. I appreciate her advice and know that she is acting in a medically responsible manner. But I know from within that I find myself right now in an entirely different context and that routine cardiac examinations would only take place in several weeks, because cardiologists have long waiting lists. Probably, they would prescribe me a tranquilizer. Only a very small amount as they always say, but enough to get hooked, is it not so? And enough to get my whole system in upheaval and confusion. But I am not to be tranquilized. I want to wake up, I want to activate my spiritual potential here on earth. Immediately, I am sure and certain that I shall not follow the osteopath´s recommendation. There must be another solution. One that corresponds to my present state. A solution for a caterpillar in its cocoon while it is undergoing a deep metamorphosis. Both the prana body and the aura are going through an exceptional transformation, and such a process demands the sovereignty of the being within as well as the respect of the various stages which naturally are very individual.

Good night.

26.04.2017 – Day 16

Five and a half hours sleep. Shortly interrupted by the well-known tachycardia. With the help of the essential oil of lavender I peacefully go back to sleep. In the morning, I enjoy my herbal tea. It is still cold, and it rains all night. I put the heating up. As already mentioned, it is unusual for me, but I found it difficult to stand the cold during the process. I try and make myself comfortable, but the palpitations are still present. I start getting annoyed at them. I do a heart programming, but I have the intuition that it is not really or not solely about my heart. What is blocked? The emotional level looks quite clear. Well, there were some very old spiritual frustrations in previous incarnations: rigid religious communities, betrayals, persecution and accusation of heresy. I look at them and can follow their effects on me. They are only mildly emotionally charged. What is otherwise missing that I do not get, I ask myself.

Suddenly the answer comes from an entirely different perspective than expected. But it does make sense.

The gallbladder has given a sign. It did bubble away yesterday evening during the treatment, but I had somehow forgotten it. It is obviously a sign that the detoxification is not complete. Then, later, after the emptying of the bowels, the heart rhythm regulates itself. Indeed, the heart was compensating all the time, because the thick gallbladder secretion caused a blockage in the solar plexus. I suddenly was freed of my tachycardia! If I had been to the doctor, he would have focused on the heart without looking for wider connections and without including other organs. The routine analysis would have led to a diagnosis that would have caused me worrying. Then I would have been sent home with a couple of pills.

Usually, the individual correlations are not taken into account and the personal needs not even looked at. But the tests are simply done according to the standard procedure. I prefer self-observation, self-responsibility and self-determination as opposed to standard treatment. Especially, as I know that my heart is basically healthy. It is of course a great advantage that I am able to measure whether ailments are really serious or whether they look worse than they are. To be honest, I did not know of such a link between heart and gallbladder, although I see the coherence from the point of view of the chakra system.

Nature shows solidarity, and when a chakra or an organ is chronically weakened, mostly the chakra which is situated above it or a neighbor organ will jump in and work for two, so that the whole system goes on functioning. In my case the heart compensated for the solar plexus chakra. I was already aware of this tendency before. But this disharmony cannot be overlooked now because of my cleansing phase.

The mental and emotional associations which I previously established are not false. Soothing the gallbladder sounds rather prosaic and concrete. We are spiritual beings. But on earth the body has the last word. Have you ever tried to meditate with a hungry or an over full stomach?

Now, I would like to go through the psychological and the further reasons behind the congested gallbladder and the overactive heart. There are always mental and emotional causes and, in a wider sense, also causal and spiritual ones, as well as ramifications with previous lives, and of course the soul ray. And why is that so? Because we are spiritual beings, whether we know it or not, whether we remember it or not. Usual treatments will hardly take these factors into consideration. I believe, it is essential and determining to know why and what we are incarnated for and which tasks we are here to fulfill. Why do I meet with topics which regularly have to do with ethics and beauty?

Well, we are making a little detour. But it is necessary to consider things in a wider perspective. So let us return to the gallbladder and its secretion. In the background of this disharmony there is the pattern of indignation. This is at the same time a family topic, particularly among the members who have been active for political and social changes. Also my mother with her revolt against her position as an economically dependent housewife stuck in her role as frustrated and hardly tolerated daughter in law. She definitely showed me what I clearly wanted to exclude from my life. Indeed, I have inherited quite a potential for indignation from my family history as well as from my incarnational experiences. And I would like to recommend the famous pamphlet by Stéphane Hessel "Time for Outrage!" in which you can read: "The worst thing is indifference." Nowadays, the head is not stuck in the sand but rather in the iphone. Edward Snowden risks his life to reveal intolerable conditions of surveillance on the greatest imaginable scale, but the majority goes on as usual. I invite you to read Vadim Zeland's last book: "Dropping out of the technogenous system" Indeed, he is one of the few spiritual persons who dare to deal with uncomfortable truths. And then the delightful booklet:" The Machine Stops" by E. M. Forster written in 1909. A small but fine literary insight into the general dulling of the mind.

How can one read an article in the New York Times about the reintroduction of torture during police interrogations in the US and particularly of waterboarding as it is still practiced in Guantanamo? The article goes on describing that it may call for the resistance of intellectuals. What a sadistic hypocrisy! And some read that for breakfast. I could literally get sick. What about you?

Another theme towards which I would like to attract the attention: Germany as the brothel of Europe. Didn´t you know? Please do google "Stop Sexkauf" and various information sources. Oh yes, it does concern you! Yes, you personally. Either because you are a man, and quite a few must be regular guests of brothels (certainly not all men), otherwise the business would not flourish the way it does. Or you are a woman and this concerns you just as well, because these women who are being tormented, tortured and humiliated there, are our sisters, women like you and me, who are living under economical pressure or have been cruelly deceived and trapped. And still more incredible: These brothels where women are being exploited sexually are only taxed approximately, in a lump sum. I myself have to provide a receipt for each amount spent or earned and I am taxed on each little thing. But the tax office only demands a general estimation of the money flow through these activities. Strange, is it not? Prostitution and pornography are making a million business and are very present in all countries that are economically successful, not only in Germany. Inform yourself and reflect about it. Open your eyes. And do act and react.

27.04.2017 – Day 17

Five and a half hours sleep, 50,5 kg, a great deal of energy.

In this metamorphosis the light body unfolds itself; it is now very receptive for the energy. I am encountering a new principle which states: the more movement and activity, the more force and power will be provided. That is completely opposite to the scarcity mentality which is typical of this society: you must be careful and keep your energy, you do not have so much strength, you are already 64!

My body is light and supple, and I get everything done in a simple and easy way. As I am moving more, my inner warmth is improving.

My opinion is that subtle supports and products may occasionally be introduced within the P.P. depending upon the individual needs. Only waiting for the effects of the light is not quite right for me. My attitude may be due to my background as a nurse, a therapist and a teacher. I know a great deal of wholistic methods that may enhance the transformation as they are themselves issued from the light consciousness. I definitely do not mean aggressive remedies which would disturb or end the BP. Who thinks they require pain killers or any other medicine should rather stop the process and have another try on a later occasion. They do not tally together.

28.04.2017 – Day 18

Today is again a very active day. I am feeling well on all levels and I am much more peaceful since my heart rhythm is regular. The weight is stable, the duration of sleep is diminishing, and I enjoy plenty of energy. These are the three criterions which stand for a successful process.

I would claim that the vitality has increased even more. It is proportional to how much it is used and spent. Energy is actually available in endless abundance and it is all about tracking it and asking for it.

A basic sensation of deep harmony is now part of my life. A profound joy and serenity have become steady companions in my life. Everything is in flow.

And I am endlessly grateful.

I have failed to mention Mimin, for she has found a comfortable place somewhere else during the rainy and snowy days. She did pay me a visit on the only nice day in the P.P.

. She came by for treatment. She just lay in the right position in front of me, and I nearly heard the instruction: „So get on with it". I gladly fulfilled her wish. As soon as the flow stops in my hands, she knows that the treatment has ended and she walks off, cleanses herself and disappears out of the garden. Done for today. I have treated her at a distance all the time, and she is now much stronger, and her eyes are not running anymore.

Before I started the P.P. I was afraid to have to go through the kidney pains again which I suffered from in my younger years. Especially during the first week ailments and illnesses that may now belong to the past are often expected to manifest themselves. This in itself is a sign of deep healing. What is chronic has to become acute. Only in this way can it be healed.

Thanks Goodness, it was not the case, for kidney complains are very painful and weakening. I shall now explain why they did not make their appearance in the present context. I had treated them thoroughly many years ago in a particular manner, which I definitely do not recommend to imitate.

At the beginning of my thirties I had already been suffering from recurrent kidney infections for years. On a couple of occasions, I took antibiotics which were not really helpful and ruined my intestinal flora. Then my teacher, who privately taught me over several years, managed to successfully treat the infections thanks to radionics. How incredibly lucky I was to have his support! I am so grateful to him up to this day! The infections became milder and rarer. Nevertheless, one day I suddenly became ill again with my kidneys. But the intervention of my teacher did not relieve my symptoms. What had been so helpful, quickly and thoroughly, on several occasions was of no help this time.

Then, I decided to let go and let God and to let the infection follow its course. Your Will be done... I was ready to die, if my body was ready for it and if it was in accordance with the Highest Will. And so, I did become very ill indeed. My organism followed an eight-hour rhythm during which fever, shivering and an exhausted sleep followed each other. That went on for seven days. Time and time again I called for the Great Force to come and collect me. My ex-husband was helpless and perplex. He could not grasp why I had chosen this way, although I worked in a naturopathic clinic. Sometimes I was lying in bed shaken by this incredible shivering with my fur coat on and begged him to lie on top of me so as to restrain the violent shaking of my body. During these seven days I had visions and recognitions as never before. I started to get acquainted with my body and its signs. I learned to trust it and I was able to let go and become more receptive for the grace. The fight against the illness and the fear of this painful body finally ended. The body and its ailments became my allies. I gave up resisting and trusted that these recurrent symptoms would stop when they had fulfilled their task. Indeed, fever and shivering stopped on the 7th day. I was weak but purified and relieved. The recovery lasted a long time, but it was very thorough, so much indeed that I have never had an infection in this area of the body again.

This experience has given me an unshakable confidence in the self-regenerative forces of the body. Let it do what it has to do. It is just trying to help you to recover and re-create the original equilibrium. Sickness is a healing strategy of the body. As I said, yes to treatment and support, but let us not disturb or block the body's own wisdom and its self-healing endeavors. It knows what it is doing. But please, this only applies to basically healthy persons, it does not apply when the system is already confused and weakened. This experience has liberated me from fears (the kidneys as organs are linked with fear patterns), it helped me gain confidence in my body by giving me the opportunity to develop a relationship with it as well as profound insights into its healing processes. It also permitted me another perspective into the power of mind over body and their interactions as well as the power of visions. This experience was an initiation in the shamanistic sense. I was never the same again.

Nature is full of regenerative forces: the trees withstand heat, cold, thunder and overcome wounds, and also wild animals recover from adversities. Dr Larry Dossey wrote a thorough report about people who could not get medically treated for their illness. After some time, many of them spontaneously became healthy again, lived and worked on and miraculously (or rather naturally) enjoyed a relatively long life. We have the possibility to make full use of the natural self-regeneration of our life force: nature is generous and favorable to life and wants to live! It is aiming at balance, re-harmonization and reestablishment of the natural, healthy order. This is in no way an encouragement not to benefit from the medical services. On the contrary! But a good deal of wisdom and trust in one's own strength actually entices the self-healing proprieties of both the mind and the body.

The fact that I had no problems with my kidneys is moreover a proof that this topic is completely solved in this incarnation. I am very grateful for this.

29.04.2017 – Day 19

I am so full of strength and nearly untiring. From morning till evening, I do my distance work as well as various daily tasks, go to the sauna, do garden work etc. Occasionally I need a little nod during the day, but after 10 to 15 minutes I am fit and fresh again. In the evening I enjoy music or some or the other concert and am surprised to develop a liking for types of music which I previously did not appreciate.

Twice a day I connect myself to the Light and tank up energy. I

share the Light with other pranic people, family and friends and build up a morphogenetic field. I pray for my family and friends, for the earth / Gaia, for humanity and all beings on the planet. Even when it is raining colors seem to be glowing. My fine hearing is shocked by the daily noise of the city, but the morning concert of the birds at 5 am fills me up with deep joy. Just the fact of experiencing the sunrise is a special treat.

30.04.2017 – Day 20

Last night was relatively long with 5 hours sleep. I have lost 600 gr this week. It makes me a little unhappy at the beginning of the day, for the weight should remain stable and the sleep should get shorter. It is true that I used to care for rather long sleeping habits before. Sleep brought me solutions and new approaches to problems. Sleep means regeneration, working freeing oneself of daily impressions, shaping future life events or developments, traveling to other dimensions and meeting their inhabitants. It does not make sense, if modern man considers sleep as a loss of time and prefers to waste his time in front of a TV or a computer rather than paying a visit to his sleep-landscapes.

Pranic sleep is shorter, more concentrated and connected to other levels of consciousness. I wake up fresh and innocent like a child after a few hours of sleep only.

Today is a wonderful, warm day and I am going on a long and steep mountain tour with a friend. It is a bit tough hiking uphill and I am short of breath. After a little nap in the grass I happily tumble down the mountain.

01.05.2017 – Day 21

Twenty first and last day of my P.P. I obtain confirmation from my guidance that the pranic transformation has successfully been completed. I program my body for a well-balanced weight. I do not want to look dry and skinny. It is possible for the body weight to gain a few hundred grams or more, as other pranics have reported.

Once again, the weather is cold, windy and rainy, which does affect me. This will certainly regulate itself. My mood is a little gloomy. Strange. Actually, today I should rejoice about the achievement and the end of the process. Which I do. But I am unable to express my joy. My mood is somewhat heavy.

Actually, my thoughts are busy with the continuation of the pranic state and how I am going to live this transformation in my daily life. The decision was clear for me from the beginning: I am going through the BP with the intention to remain in this pranic modus for an indefinite period of time. That is now my modus operandi. Except in case of illness or in case of an inner impulse or if my Highest Instance would instruct me differently, only in these exceptional cases I would go back to a solid, material way of nourishment.

I enjoy much more time for myself through the fact that I need less sleep and that the whole food preparation rituals are cancelled (shopping, cooking, eating, washing up and tiding up the kitchen). Now the question is how I am to make use of this newly recovered time factor in a purposeful and meaningful manner in the long run. Right now, I am a little empty and slightly at a loss. It is like a vacuum that wants to be reflected upon, given a new orientation and filled up. Maybe not ..., says another aspect of myself. It is not only a matter of time, but it has to do with energy which is now available together with a great impulse to get moving. An interesting situation.

Now the cells know that they are loading up the Light and charging themselves to go on living. The aura and the physical body are altered and connected to a more subtle food source. This complete state of being still wants to be stabilized and especially lived and experienced in daily life with all the chances and challenges which my life is offering me.

PART TWO: MY GENERAL CONDITION AFTER THE INSTALLATION

On 01.05.2017 my P.P. came to an end after 3 weeks of prana installation. As I am intending to maintain the pranic state, I now share my further development at random dates for the coming months up to the 11th April 2018. By then, it will be a whole year living on Light while leading a normal working, social and private life.

07.05.2017

Prana has been installed for a week now. I am feeling well. I am feeling less cold when I sometimes drink coffee. Unfortunately, the weather remains gloomy and rainy, so that I am rather tired and not feeling very motivated. Pranic sleep is wonderful. Going to sleep and waking up is so light, gentle and clear like sliding from one state into the next. But also, very refreshing so that four to five hours are sufficient.

The drive to move is strong and I often get up early for a long walk in the park, sometimes even under the rain. I enjoy the elements: freshness, wind, air fulfill me with happiness and nurture me.

Unfortunately, I have lost some more weight, which is not advantageous for my small stature.

I feel I am still in an in-between phase, during which I am taking good care of myself, and I am still avoiding too many people. Soon I shall visit my family and friends again. I shall tell them about the essence of the process as simply and as clearly as possible. I have opted for another way of nourishing myself like somebody who is vegetarian and then decides to become vegan. This person is still nourishing herself from something, but on a more subtle alimentation. I used to drink smoothies and now I am feeding on light. Indeed, even though I am not eating any nourishment of some sort. Of course, for someone who knows nothing about the subtle worlds it may sound a little abstract. But it can also be a stimulus to think anew or discover something new, if one is ready.

11.07.2017

Exactly three months ago I started with the P.P. Today I am on a wonderful mountain tour in the Engadin. As I wake up, I am not feeling too well. My stomach is aching. I should be going to the toilet. It does not happen often anymore. And it needs a certain preparation somehow. When it is done, I feel well, light and clear. Then the day starts. Today I am only taking a little honey and I have a lot of strength and endurance. I do not feel any fatigue until late in the night. The body is light and vital and enjoys the movement. The activity fills it up with life force and it charges itself with Light. I am also inspired intellectually, and I am quite productive.

Today is a perfect confirmation of my breatharian experiment. It is a present of the new spirit, a transformation which provides me with me a new life. I am full of gratefulness. My body is getting stronger, more resistant and endurance: I feel no fatigue at all after the difficult mountain walk. On the contrary,

I am quite refreshed. On other levels I am stable with a good ability to maintain healthy boundaries. The night with its five hours of sleep or less is enough and always very regenerating. I do not even need a little nod during the day. I enjoy a good, balanced vitality without speeding up, as it was the case at the beginning of the P.P.

24.07.2017

In the last few days my body has been rebelling and I am suffering from the weight loss and its symptoms. This morning I am not feeling well, although I have already taken honey in lukewarm water. I suppose that my weight has reached its lowest safe limit and that is why it is ringing the alarm-bell. As a matter of fact, it is not a supposition but a fact, for its signs are clearer and stronger than ever. Of course, I did what was appropriate in this situation and I could do my work properly and with all my senses.

Because of the activity of the digestive system, I am feeling tired this evening, but I am more relaxed. Right now, I am adding some honey to my herbal tea. Like during fasting I am lapping up my drinks or I let a little honey melt on my tongue. I am still keeping my connection to the Light and I am doing my physical exercises as usual. During the coming night I may need more sleep, which is often the case when I take honey to reduce the weight loss.

So I continue the pranic state, but I am intending to gain a bit more mass and keep the weight stable. At the same time, I am adamant to retaining the awareness of pranism and that I do not fall back into the so called "normal state", which would feel rather "heavy and slow".

Today Mimin comes for her treatment. She is tense. Actually, she does not feel well, and she is in pain. She is restless and wants to leave again. Yet she hangs around a little longer and makes me understand telepathically that she will visit me once more before she passes away. Then she goes her way, completely detached. Have I understood properly? I feel terribly sad and let a couple of tears run down my cheek. Nevertheless, it is a wonder that Mimin is still alive. It is obvious that her life force is diminishing. When will she visit me next?

08.09.2017

In three days-time I shall reach the five months and I am still not living purely from water and air. I enjoy plenty of energy, strength and lust for venture and inspiration as well as an inner guidance which is particularly clear and perceptible these days. My need for sleep is still reduced. My link to prana is more alive and direct and increasingly more integrated on the cellular level than earlier. My intellectual abilities are faster and more profound. My capacity to see behind the facades and behavior patterns is without compromise. A lot of things have become easier and simpler and my inner world is more satisfied and coherent. I feel very courageous and even more resolute than before. The spiritual path is not an afternoon walk. It demands the true practice of freedom with the complete responsibility which goes with it. Some friends are giving up their friendship to me; relationships which were previously harmonious are now less peaceful or even have a break, at least for the moment. It is good so. People have the right to take a break.

By the way, I have dealt with the topic "fear of losing weight". At first, I rejected the theory of "losing weight, because I was afraid to lose weight", as a simple assumption which could be applied to everybody and anybody. To a certain degree it does sound like a sweeping statement. But it is still worth analyzing and verifying from a personal point of view. Indeed, I do not want to look like a bunch of bones with dried sunken features. I come in touch with a lot of people, travel and work a lot and I care for my appearance and the vibration which I leave as an imprint in this world.

What is even more important to me is how I am feeling. The detoxification lasts on further than the 21-day transformation process. From time to time, I compensate my sensitivity to the cold and the weight loss with a little fresh cream.

Of course, I occasionally know fear or apprehension, for example, when I am preparing myself for a professional journey or an appearance in public. The signs associated with the weight loss make me uncertain and draw my whole attention upon them. I cannot afford to be distracted by them, when I am teaching, holding a conference or giving a session. In those moments, I do need to direct my whole concentration on the client or the audience. So I see it as my responsibility to get everything that is required done, previously and in time, so as to be a neutral medium and completely present for my clients. It is obvious that in this case anticipation is playing a role on my part. In fact, I avoid putting myself into an unwished-for situation.

This is no new experience for me, for 20 years ago I was very thin, and a naturopath advised me to take in fluid cream. It looks as if my metabolism is very active and quickly tends to burn fats. Sometimes a little sesame purée is a good alternative for me, but no olive or linseed oil, as some occasionally suggest.

It is a matter of finding out what the specific requirements of this unique body are, and not to follow whatever theory or fashion. I would encourage each and every one to weigh out what is right, helpful, and what makes sense for him/her at the present moment. And this of course does not apply only to pranic people but obviously to each and everyone.

I stand for prana made to measure. That means not letting oneself be squeezed into a set up format. No Procrustes' bed. It does not mean either to get into a competition with the lucky ones who manage to give up eating and drinking from one day to the other. Good for them. For me it is a little different.

The majority of people doing the P.P. will sooner or later give up pranic alimentation and go back to usual solid foods - either for private, psychological, social or for physical reasons.

I am meditating in the garden with my legs up. I am in such a deep state that I do not notice Mimin. She jumps up on my lap, which makes me emit a short cry of surprise, which again scares her. So she jumps back onto the grass. She is not well. Suddenly, the weather changes and it starts raining. Exceptionally, I let her inside the apartment. She chooses the best and most comfortable place to sleep. I have to get something from town. For a short moment I wonder whether I should leave her alone inside. I know she does not like being locked in. It is raining heavily, and I cannot throw out an old animal that is ill. Anyway, she is sleeping deeply and does not let herself be disturbed. After shopping I am glad to come home to find Mimin. Maybe she is feeling better and wants to sit on my lap and be stroked for a while.

No, Mimin does not. As I open the door, she walks out the apartment door, completely detached and unconcerned. Then I get a shock: at first sight, the flat looks devastated. What happened? Both curtains, two meters high, which were hanging at the door window giving onto the garden now lay across the floor together with other objects. Yes, the curtains which I was too lazy to get down and wash last week. Well, now everything is on the floor: the curtains including their rod, as well as everything else that layed in their way. I notice the trace of claws on the material which is partly damaged. Indeed, she tried to get out through the garden door as usual. It is impossible to get angry at her. It must have been a shock for her anyway!

13.09.2017

Today I sense that Mimin's aura does not belong to the terrestrial plane. At first, I cannot accept it. I test my impression. Indeed, she has gone to the other worlds. So that had been her very last visit. I want to know how she died and ask one of the neighbors who has been feeding her. "She's gone." "How, gone?" "Wiped off, her owner took her to the vet." Would it not be possible to speak a little more respectfully of an animal that one has fed for years? "Thanks for the info." I go away. My heart is oppressed and tight. Since then I have followed Mimin further on. For a long time, she did not find peace beyond, either. I say farewell to this dear being that was incarnated in a cat's body.

Let go and go on living. But experiences linger on and remain, ingrained, even when the landscapes, the actors and the life sequences follow upon each other and dissolve. Luckily, my P.P. has not left such a disturbance in the apartment. It is easier for me to give up material food than to let go of Mimin.

03.11.2017

Nearly seven months ago my new life with prana started. The last couple of days I have not been feeling too well because of the cold. I feel thin and vulnerable, physically and mentally. I am tired. I need more sleep. I have little reserve: too many demands, too much discipline. Indeed, I set very high standards to myself and I have added a lot of exercises to a multitude of professional duties. Now I am listless. Actually, it is not so dramatic, but my summer overactivity is definitely over.

I do not look good, my cheeks are sunken in, the wrinkles more visible. The scales are confirming the weight loss, although my weight had been stable all that time. Ok, so nothing new. Again, I take honey, which slightly reduces the vibration of the pranic state and makes sleep a little longer. Well, winter modus is on: well wrapped up, sleepy and sucking honey. Already, after a couple of days my appearance improves.

Then I get the idea of testing vitamins, trace elements and minerals in my body. I want to know, whether all main nutrients are present. Yes, the Light is providing me with everything I require. My measurements confirm it. I am not lacking anything. I am glad to be able to know this with certainty. Later, I test a few of my clients and notice that several are lacking at least one or two nutrients, although they eat normally.

I am used to my pranic state now and it is nothing exceptional anymore. From time to time somebody asks when I shall end my process and eat normally again. I answer that my feeding on Light is nurturing and nourishing for me, that I am getting on well and that I see no reason why I should give it up.

10.12.2017

In September this is my fifth month as a pranic person I decide to have my teeth attended to. I patients. On the following day I. However, I immediately went to work and drank too little water. That is why I must catch up today with the good water from the osmosis appliance from the firm Weber Bio-Energie Systeme (weberbio,de). With "good water", I mean water that is alive and has been and freed of the usual poisons and hormones, antidepressants etc. as they are found in the drinking water of all big cities. In the case of osmotic water, the wall of the water molecules is permeable and it therefore optimally serves the detoxifying of cellular tissues in the body. But, of course, I must drink sufficiently. I follow the cleansing process of the kidneys by observing the smell, color and density of the urine. Besides, I absolutely need to move, which is typical for me when I am not feeling well. Right now, it is an issue, because I find it hard to walk straight due of the dizziness. I probably look like a slightly drunk woman. Nobody would ever believe that the cause of it is purely a dental treatment! So first of all, let us get the system rinsed through with enough fluids, then off I go! I quickly recover from this little episode. After three months of intensive work the lady dentist completes her excellent job. In the following days I track the elimination of the used remedies through skin, urine, stool and the smell of the body. To re-establish the alkaline ph-balance of the body and sustain the cleansing I drink water with fresh lemon juice and honey. Movement in the fresh air and purifying baths complete my program.

I am very grateful that the treatment was so successful and that my pranic body has dealt so well with the situation. I told the lady dentist of my breatharian modus only at the end of the treatment.

13.12.2017

The winter's cold in Germany is a problem for me.

As soon as the autumn started, my body reacted with oversensitivity to the uncomfortable dropping temperatures. The memory of the spring cold is still present in the cells. The weight loss and the somewhat slower blood circulation are causing this oversensitivity. I wonder whether it would make sense to emigrate to one of the many colonies. No, they are not called colonies anymore. But the traces of the French megalomania are still present, and I could not live there with good and clear conscience. Besides, the original population lives there in very poor conditions. Precarious and rootless in their own lost paradise. Do not the inhabitants of Madagascar count among the people with the lowest BIP in the word? So this thought quickly ended the topic of emigration. The deep connections which I have developed and woven with Germany, with its language and with the German people over the decades cannot be dissolved just like that. The longing for warmth is not sufficient to let me leave a country and its people who are so dear to me. I cannot separate my profound development and evolution from this country. I benefit here from certain qualities and opportunities that contribute to my spiritual path. In the German speaking area, I feel accepted as I am and I enjoy the proper resonance with my surroundings. I like the people and their reliability. I am grateful to be allowed to live where it pleases me.

Good, then I shall stay here. I just need warm clothing, especially warm shoes. Already in the spring I developed good habits and I care for my body so as to keep it healthy and warm. Besides, I now use spices which generate warmth like cinnamon or ginger and make hot teas with them to which I add a little honey. In no case may the water be too hot, otherwise it destroys the positive qualities of the honey and transforms them into a disadvantageous chemical mixture in the body, so the ayurvedic teachings say.

I am doing all I can to train my body to be resistant and capable of generating its own warmth. The contrast warm/cold is stimulating: As soon as I get up, I go barefoot in the garden, even if there is snow. Then I dry my feet and pack them into warm socks. The whole being enjoys this, and it fortifies and stabilizes the blood circulation. Alternating warm-cold showers are also healthy and beneficial. They strengthen the immune system. Thank God, I have a comfortable, pleasant apartment, warm clothes and everything I need. How lucky I am! Only 10% of humanity lives in this abundance. And I belong to it! It is a challenge to make something special out of this situation, is it not? Being grateful is the first step.

In addition to the stimulating effect of the warm-cold alternation I am adamant about my flat not being too warm. I prefer to wear several layers of clothing and if needed two pairs of socks to walking around in a T-shirt in an overheated room, where the mucous membranes of the nose, the hair and the skin dry up, the mind is getting lethargic and confused and the too comfortable body is getting lazy.

I take care of my metabolism and prevent it from getting too thin. I occasionally add a little sesame puree to the honey to get some fat and to counteract my sensitivity to the cold. I suffered quite a bit in the spring and now I develop an appropriate strategy. Honey does not interrupt the pranic state which is well established in the meantime.

A further point which I considered in spring during my P.P. is the constant obsession with and the fear of the cold. One talks about how cold it is now or how cold it once was at whatever occasion. The unpleasantness of the situation is being magnified by the apprehension and the negative expectation. But the chilblain does not get better or feel better through concentrating on it being a chilblain. On the contrary, I do my best not to become a victim of a loop in my thinking but rather to learn to project a healthy body-reaction into the future and I also train my organism, adopt good habits and develop a sound resistance. It all provides me with a sturdy life force. And I am also psychically better prepared and less dependent upon outer thermal variability.

Through the transformation I have become more receptive to the changing quality of the weather. Mood, body tissues, bones, body fluids, articulations, cold temperature and sleep:

even if they do not react all together all the time and in the same intensity, I am definitely more receptive to thermic and atmospheric pressures. My organism even registers a few degrees less, and the bones take on the dampness in a fine and subtle manner which cannot be ignored. In other words, I have become a human barometer, not only for the weather, but also for the vibrations of the day: When I listen within, I can feel which activities are favorable and make sense on which day. Then everything wonderfully flows, and I can get a lot of work done, physically as well as intellectually. I find myself in the flow, in alignment with myself and with the frequency of the day. Each day is unique and consequently the result and the carrier of various influences, whether they are cosmic, astrological, atmospheric, energetic, political, psychic etc., only to mention a few streams which now come to mind. There are many more influences of the inner as well as outer realms, known and unknown which variously modulate, motivate or tune us. Early in the morning, I feel within the energy of the day as well as my state of mind. It is then my intention to intuitively find out the energy stream that flows best and is most harmonious, productive and creative. It is all about latching my Higher Self onto the Highest Good and hooking into this alignment. All kinds of appointments, duties etc. render the game more complicated, but it is an art in itself to master the day and simultaneously remaining oneself. I have given up a lot of things that are uninteresting or meaningless for me. Life is too precious to waste it with activities or people with which I have no or little resonance.

This is a highly concentrated winter and I am clearing out on all levels. Nothing new for me. Exactly as I need no more solid food there are many things which I do not need any more. I have renewed the arrangement of the furniture in my small apartment. Now I have more space to move. And emptiness, empty shelves, empty tables, empty walls.

I fell on the ice. I now have a big bruise on the left elbow. It looks ugly but I do not feel any pain. I am grateful for this heavy fall, for it is a proof that I do not suffer from osteoporosis. The healing process went very well. It is a pleasure to realize how well my body is reacting and regenerating itself in the eighth month of pranic living. In this context, I can also mention that other small wounds like a cut on my finger or an infection on my toe healed rapidly and thoroughly. The blood coagulation rate is also perfect.

I now wish to mention a spice which is very helpful in the wintertime because of its warming effect: cinnamon. Moreover, it possesses several other proprieties: On the one side it livens up and stabilizes the blood circulation and cleanses the bowels, on the other side it provides concentration and clear thinking. I appreciate its effects as well as its taste and mix it up with warm water and honey to make an excellent winter drink.

Of course, I take care of my health. I treat myself with informative energies which I have developed out of various systems. I also do regular check-ups to test my state in an objective manner. I still enjoy a lot of strength, but it is rather in a normal range now, not like in the summertime when I was really fired off by the planet Mars. I experience the winter atmosphere as I usually know it: introverted with longer sleep phases, the need for peace and quiet and a passion for study.

As intended, I have put on weight against the cold. Once again, I am having a big cleanse on several levels: from my scalp down to an infected toe; the tongue is covered, the skin shows a couple of red patches and my intestines are emptying themselves in a fluid manner. The body wants to get rid of these small infections which we tend to carry latently and unnoticed with us, especially when we are older. That is why I welcome these reactions of my body.

January 2018

Except for the cold I did not meet with big challenges in January. Nevertheless, I decided to buy myself proper winter clothing and shoes. It spares me from freezing and complaining.

As my blood circulation was a bit unstable, I have resumed sauna visits. I used to be a passionate sauna goer over decades, but I renounced it as I started the P.P. My good and dear body is enjoying the warm air and the water. It is even perspiring which is a rather unusual reaction in my present state. How good! On this first occasion, I am not forcing myself to go into the cold basin or to go under the cold shower. But I am confident that I shall soon jump into it, as I used to. For this first time the three goes in the sauna are sufficient to get my blood pressure to the right level. Now I feel how the blood is reaching into fingers and toes. It is the appropriate moment to make a big compliment to my body and to thank it for the numerous adventures through which it has accompanied me, especially during this last experiment. I find it fascinating how the practical knowledge and the memory of the sauna are so well stored in the cells and how easily they can get called up again. Not only concerning the sweating but also various physical exercises and trainings. In the past, I was partly very hard with my body, I neglected it, ignored its reactions, just wanted it to function and me be like the others. I have fed it badly, in spite of demanding a lot of it as I worked hard. I have abruptly ended up long fasting periods although I knew better. I took the functioning body for granted-without gratefulness and appreciation. He has given his best without complaining much. A couple of times he became acutely ill but did not react well to allopathic medicine. But he showed me new and different ways which paved and supported my life since. Parallel to this I developed confidence in him and in my researches. I know it is always right. There is only one thing that he never liked: drugs, legal or illegal, strong medicine, poisons and alcohol. He always reacted vehemently to these substances. Today I am grateful to him for it. I had to vomit and had terrible headaches. While the others seem to be in heaven, I was kneeling down, bent over the toilet bowl and hated myself for it, because I was not even able to hang around with these people. Where do I fit in on this earth, I wondered? Nowhere, was my answer. After admitting this I started behaving as if I was a guest on this planet. Also, as a visitor you can feel well, even if a few things seem strange, but at least many are interesting and even fascinating. I am still here. This is a wonder in itself, and the way I am feeling right now I dare say it will go on a few more years until my stay comes to an end on this earth. In a pranic state.

Maybe you also feel like saying "Thank you" to your body. This is your vehicle with which you navigate in this dimension. Be good to it. It will be grateful and serve you well.

If I want to sum up my present condition I can clearly confirm: the longer the Light nourishment, the better, for I have reached the ninth month in January.

There is an observation which I have not yet mentioned. It is the fact that my libido has been switched off together with the increase of Light within the cells. I have not yet read in any report that the pranic modus would sedate sexual functions. I bet there will be at least 20 virile men who have been living pranically for the last decades and who will disclaim my assumption and confirm the opposite effect! Well, I am solely reporting my own modest experience here! I even have discovered more precious phenomenons: New antennas are growing out of all pores and I enjoy and appreciate my surroundings even more. My perception is finer and acuter, and to my experience my sensations are more intense and deeper Many people and objects are radiating and sending out Light in/to their surroundings. I am fascinated by the various nuances of the lady's black garment who is sitting across me. The consistence of the black color offers so many more variations than I had realized before. The whole of life is so much richer in its nuances. My intuition and my intellect are more awake and clearer, and I feel much more fulfilled than before the P.P. My ability to manifest has improved, I am more consequent and more authentic which is not always easy for my surroundings. To confront oneself with truth is something for courageous souls, for it is easier to float in a sea of illusion and at the surface of the general consensus. Is it not urgent to go deeper and recognize the truth and stand up to one´s convictions, right now? Do not believe it is always easy for me, either. I am pushed to my limits and thoroughly confronted with the human condition. But what is right and fair and in accordance with the Highest Good will sooner or later be recognized as the ultimate word. This is embodied by and through the heart, through empathy, enthusiasm (in the original meaning of the ancient Greek word "enthousiazen" which means, inspired by God and grace. And also, through clarity of thinking, feeling and perceiving through the antennae of the aura.

February 2018

My eyesight has rather improved through the techniques that I have been practicing. Already several decades ago I noticed that seeing is thoroughly dependent upon the psyche and its latent and changing moods. Do observe your eyes and their functioning in correlation with your attitudes, your moods and your processes. You will gain a lot of in-sights that will help you to see through things and maybe even see things through. It is not only a matter of diopter: the sense of sight also fluctuates with emotional and mental variations. What do you think about it? Anyway, reading the timetables in tiny print without glasses is over for me; at least, on most days and especially when in a hurry.

In February there are a few disharmonies with orders, delivery services and teamwork with colleagues. With time, good will and common effort we manage to attain satisfying solutions.

Now there is a clearing phase in the interaction with friends, acquaintances and professional partners, either on the ground of their personal situation or initiated through my instigation. I need concentrated, purposeful and enriching exchanges. Or stillness, meditation, going within, but no superficial stuff devoid of content.

Some relationships have gained a positive development and have become deeper and more essential in their essence. Nurturing, reliable connections to friends and colleges are for me a true source of fulfillment. I am deeply grateful for them.

The increased Light within my cells is generating clearing and change. Moreover, the position of both planets, Jupiter and Saturn – one oriented within, the other without – mirrors this strong polarization. They are slowly approaching each other until the 21st of December 2020, when the so called "big conjuncture" is taking place, and that happens only once in twenty years. The last time was in the year 2000. Generally, Saturn is being considered as having a hindering and limiting effect and is usually negatively interpreted; even good astrologists fear its negative influence. This is a shame. Even if I am not an astrologist and only have limited knowledge of this ancient science, I would like to make a certain contribution. I was confronted with its effects when I was 28, and my conception of the world was shaken upside down. I became seriously ill, confused and suddenly had uncontrolled perceptions which opened up new dimensions for me. I got rattled and had to wake up. I had to accept my clairvoyance and use it to serve people and life as a whole. Saturn became my ally. To make friends with Saturn means to agree with the Highest Will, to accept it, to give in devotion, in freedom and dignity, in order to co-create with him. Saturn deals with particular themes and asks unpleasant questions, such as: Do you live in alignment with your soul, with the plan? Does your journey tally with your soul's intent? His influence compels one to re-consider what is not in accordance, what is not valid anymore and to confront what one would rather tend to avoid or overvalue. Saturn seems to know our deepest vulnerability. He seems to let it surface and, if it has to be, he is an expert in setting limits and borders. He is a strict teacher. But if one is able to understand and assimilate the deeper meaning of the conflict, and if one is able to integrate the changes in thinking and in behavior on a daily basis, his reward is generous. In my case he led me to my vocation. The price is high for the ego and may be associated with loss, confrontation and the necessity to assert oneself. The lesson of this planet is nevertheless always a learning-task and never a punishment as opposed to what is often experienced or even claimed. Indeed, he forces one to go within, to look in depth, to clear out without compromise all that is untrue, not valid, or superficial. Yes, his task is to awaken. His influence will be felt even more sharply, because Jupiter stands in conjunction with him. And Jupiter likes no limits and limitations; quite on the contrary, he wants to expand, go out into the world to announce truth and freedom. How should they get on with each other? Not at all, if one only sees them as opposites. But yes, indeed! There do exist possibilities in spite of given limits and restrictions to let go of heaviness and to fly off to higher freedom and fulfill the commitment to the soul's mission.

This is where I detect my chances, even if the tearing apart of both planets seems unbearable and at times touches upon the substance.

But I am asking you: What are we here for? Here, incarnated in the 21st century with our growing consciousness?

We are getting to a point where the old rules are not valid anymore, where things cannot go on as they have done; a new order is coming into being. May it be in the truth, in accordance with the world-soul serving each and every being in alignment with the Highest Good.

People with strong Jupiter/Saturn aspects will be more affected by their conjunction. Everything and everybody is receptive to their transformative imprints. We can benefit either from them, reach and discover new shores, or we live with the impression of being the victims of meaningless, arbitrary coincidences.

The last challenge of this special Jupiter-Saturn relationship is that the first is oriented towards the outside, the second one rather inwards. Basically, they have completely opposed directions. Whenever the psyche is in a disharmonious condition the person feels torn apart and surrounded by inner and outer conflicts. In a balanced state it is appropriate to know one's own healthy boundaries and at the same time to recognize the necessity of both tendencies. In an optimal situation an authentic connection or bridge gets built between the esoteric dimension, that is, the inner, hidden aspects and the exoteric one, that is, the outward and extroverted aspects of the being and of life. This is indeed balance or harmony. Nevertheless, before this aim is reached, it is obvious that some oscillations and detours may lead us astray. Moreover, I would like to explain one more aspect of this conjunction, namely the co-habitation of freedom (Jupiter) and discipline (Saturn) which, when it is well-balanced, can foster a greater capacity of self-determination. In any case, it is fascinating to witness the evolution within the being and its transformational force on society.

Movement creates warmth. I need more movement. I buy myself a trampoline to get rid of my overflow of energy in a healthy and meaningful way. It offers me a more differentiated training field than my other power routine I shall keep it up further on but maybe only three times a week. But I need a balance to the strength training. Jumping on the trampoline contributes to my well-being for it loosens the fascies and activates the lymphatic system. Could it have something to do with our two planets? The optimal purpose which is engendered by two contrary modalities, joins, unifies and transcends them. Do observe this pattern in other domains also!

The pranic state is still part of my daily living. Clarity and clearing on all levels is an effect of Light in the different parts of my life. Parallel to that function it is also directing its rays on what is not clear, on the confusion: contradictions, not logical, incoherent thinking and behavior as well as illusion. In some cases, it unravels things that are unfair or manipulative, so that justice wins. That was my favorite topic during childhood. Sometimes I was tormented and kept awake at night by a situation where ethics and honesty were not applied. Time and time again I have been confronted by these themes, and time and time again I come to the same conclusion: „Keep to your own truth, be honest!" even if the price is high like rejection, punishment and loss. Nevertheless, this is only the illusion of the very moment. In the long run truth always wins. The child in me already knew that.

Sometimes I am asked: „Are you allowed to drink this or that?" Vegetarians and vegans also encounter this phenomenon. A particular foodstuff is identified as specially bad or forbidden and sets off the control question with many question marks. Pranism as well as other conversions to a different kind of diet have nothing to do with "being allowed or not" – except in the case of health problems where particular foodstuff should be avoided, like for example sugar with diabetes. As far as prana, vegetarianism and veganism are concerned it is a matter of consciousness and self-responsibility. Of course, the body reactions are decisive. One can hardly oversee them. At least I cannot!

March 2018

On the whole I have well overcome the cold-wave. I visited a friend in the mountains. It was so cold at times, that I even sucked the little chocolate that is often being served with the hot drinks you order. Not only does it taste fine, but it provides me with the lacking warmth. But each time I eat it I feel how it makes my vibration sink and how it makes me rather heavy. And the worst happens even later, when I notice that my digestive organs cannot deal with the chocolate. It actually pollutes my system and I feel unwell for a couple of days until the sweet temptation is eliminated by my organism and out of my system.

The consequence of which is that I get seized by a cleaning and purifying urge: I have cleansing baths, drink ginger-water etc. It does not take long until there is a reaction. Sudden and strong symptoms of elimination take over my skin and my intestines, which in itself is a good thing, if only a little too good. My body is very receptive and reacts very directly and intensely to impulses. I must make a note of this increased receptivity and reactivity and remember it on future occasions. Saturn and the body are defending their boundaries. Ok, I have understood the lesson and shall act accordingly.

When I suffer from the cold, I think of people who are sleeping outside. Of course, I do not know them all, but I noticed the Roma people from Rumania. They are often begging and are despised by many here. Are they really so well organized in mafia gangs to trick the money out of the citizens´ pockets as the newspapers like to claim? Communication with them is complicated through the fact that Roma people rarely speak German. But I manage to make out that some of them have been stranded here for years already because they have no official papers. Some of them should gather the money for the journey back home from their begging activity. Of course, it is obvious that they are somehow organized. One does not need to be a sociologist to guess that a kind of hierarchy rules among them, where one person or a small group controls and exploits the others. But is not our wonderful society also based on this pattern? In any case, it is not heroic to humiliate the weakest and the poorest and to peck at their last bit of dignity. And that is quite a bit. Because it contains the divine spark which is pulsating in you and me. Precisely the same. Please do feel within it deep down. It is the perception of this shared and common humanity that forces me, in spite of the cold, to pull myself together, prepare flasks of hot chai (Romas´favorite drink) and many self-made sandwiches and to take the underground to one of the places where they often gather. Their fingers swollen and frozen from the cold can hardly hold the cup and the sandwich. Yes, they have spent several nights outside at temperatures below zero. I mainly address myself to the women who, like everywhere else, have to carry the heaviest load, as they are most endangered in their human dignity due to the patriarchal structures which also exits among the Roma people. Sometimes we manage to communicate with each other, and a kind of exchange takes place with a little Italian or even Russian. A smile, comprehension, humanness, and already they are no more anonymous begging people, on the contrary, each one has his/her own smile, his/her own way of being, his/her own personality, his/her own story. Actually, I do learn a great deal through the exchanges with them, mostly without words. I respect them.

What does it all have to do with breatharianism? Before the process I was compassionate. Now it concerns me even more, for the Light opens the heart. No sweet talk, quite on the contrary, I am allergic to it. Let the reservoirs of love overflow and let it spread into the world. The wisdom of the open heart immediately senses that which is not in order and that which does not correspond to the truth, even if we have got used to certain conditions and taken habits which we consider "normal" and take for granted. We end up tolerating intolerable things.

Every day I invoke the Highest Light and pray that injustice be uncovered, and that equity be restored. This morning I shall go to these people again who are outside in the cold and the snow.

My feeding on Light is still the right diet for me. It has now become normal for me and I do not miss anything. My life has changed, it is filled up with sensual impressions, with intellectual, spiritual, deep and inspiring insights about myself and other beings. I have now been pranic for the last eleven months, and it is steadily getting better. My condition is stable and resistant. I am very active and work a great deal. According to my last measurements I am not lacking anything, and my subjective impression confirms it. The sleep duration has reduced itself to 4 hours a night and I enjoy a little nap during the day, if I can.

09.04.2018

There are several reasons why my notices have become rarer lately: First of all, because my pranic way of life is now thoroughly integrated in my daily life. Secondly, because I am journeying more and more deeply into an intensive phase of internalization. I feel introverted and highly focused, I tend to be laconic, only giving short answers and avoiding conversations which do not have to be. At the moment I cannot stand silliness, gossip, detours, distraction, trivial and watered-down communication. Luckily, I am surrounded by wonderful, reliable people who also appreciate sound and substantial communication. Not that our exchange is exclusively businesslike, but we practice a certain clarity in our intentions as well as reliability and well-aimed expression. And reciprocal respect, appreciation and understanding do not require constant and superficial "proof of love". I feel at ease with this way of relating: free, authentic and loyal. I feel accepted for who I am, and I also accept others as they are. Time and time again, we enjoy a wonderful cooperative and mutually supporting interaction based on each other's appreciation.

At the moment, I take the freedom to go into a radical withdrawal. In other words, I have to. Although I am busy with all sorts of energetic researches and find myself on an inner journey, there is nothing concrete to tell at the moment.

I am searching, I do not know exactly for what, even if again and again I receive tipps and inspirations like the pieces of a puzzle which want to be put together from fragments into a plausible picture. In the stillness lie the answers and the new ideas.

I am well acquainted with these phases of introversion, I have already had several similar experiences. In the past I misunderstood what was happening and forced myself to undertake something, to go outward and to be active. Just act "normally", just appear to be "normal"! In my youth I also feared to get I feared to get pulled into an introverted undertow, which was a realistic assumption, as I would claim nowadays. Only 15 years ago, an Imam, a wise eastern person, gave me an explanation for these recurrent need for inner withdrawal. At least one that made sense to me. In his rudimentary German he told me I was a derwish (a mystic) like him and that we sometimes have to be entirely quiet, that we do not want to talk and that we can only attend to the minimum. Like a hermit he used to go completely within during these periods, took no food, did not communicate with anybody, could not tolerate any disturbance, in order to cultivate stillness and be with it and be receptive for the inner voice and any inspired intuitions. In his position and as man he would be respected by his community and was allowed to reduce his social duties to a minimum.

I am dealing with the situation in a different modus, but I am now able to follow the inner call without personal conflict.

And now I wish to share something that has just taken place at this very moment with my readers. An acquaintance of mine, Gertrud, who I only see about once a year, has just walked in the shop unexpectedly. She tells me about the Cathars and how some of them lived without solid, material food after they had received a special blessing. This is an answer to a question which I did have, but could not answer myself. Indeed, it seems possible that initiated Cathars were living on Light. Did I practice it already in a past incarnation?

At this point I would like to address two more topics. I have adapted my meditation to my active way of life. Visualization now occupies more importance and particularly the perception with the felt sense of the light in the body as well as in the aura. I can practice it everywhere, also while moving and jumping on my trampoline. This is a practical integration of meditation into daily life.

Last month I had once more an intensive cleansing crisis which I induced through special bathes and teas. The results were multiple and very pronounced. These symptoms are the expression of poisons and other waste products which got stored over the decades and now find their way out of the tissues. At any rate, such reactions should not be stopped or repressed. They are part of the self-cleansing system which regenerates itself and which resumes its function once more under optimal conditions. What a wonder, is it not? Nevertheless, it demands the ability to understand and to cope with it instead of just being afraid. Indeed, some of these crises can be acute. Doctors and other therapists should be able to teach their patients about them, enabling mothers to treat and care for their children during acute cleansing phases with respect and attention not only for the body but for the whole being Then we would all have a strong immunity, less illness and more healthy citizens. Fever is a very useful reaction of your body. Indeed, fever is a natural antibiotic. Most viruses get destroyed by fever from 39,5°C onwards. Why do we systematically want to reduce fever? To allow the viruses to do their own thing? To weaken the human system? Could somebody give me a plausible, scientific answer? No, I had no fever, but I had other signs of depuration. Good so. Whatever is outside the body, is not being stored inside anymore. I feel that my system is quite clear and cleansed at this stage.

On another level I had insights into our sisterly mechanisms, which were at first sight really surprising to me – especially as I had been involved into them for decades and always took them for granted: I let myself be manipulated by the way of seeing and perceiving another person. The result of the situation is biased and unfair. Suddenly I woke up. It is a good thing to unknot such an old story and to clear it with the concerned persons. That is the way Light functions. Like a spotlight it makes everything visible, also habits and points of view which have solidified over years. But one does not have to be a breatharian to benefit from its discerning and clearing effects. The intensive Light does its work on earth unseen by the majority, misinterpreted by many. It is important to hold the kaleidoscope to the Light time and time again. Also it helps to get a glimpse of the new constellations being born, so that one can anchor them in one's consciousness.

11.04.2018

Exactly a year ago I started I started my P.P.. I have spent a whole year as a pranic person of grade 3, that means that I belong to the breatharians, who do not consume solids but take fluids (water, herbal teas, coffee) and occasionally honey. Pranic persons who still rarely drink a little water and otherwise have completely renounced material food – for at least four months – belong to grade four.

These are the informations which the public is interested in. But as you already know, basically something else matters: namely consciousness, awareness as well as being able to think differently. One thing is certain: I shall not let myself be tested, weighed, observed or even registered. Such measures are inappropriate for the pranic way of life and other complementary themes as well.

Any kind of blinder and prejudices are inadequate and so is the attitude or the spirit (or lack of it) which those measures are dealt with. The conviction that something cannot or should not be will justify all means to prove it. Doubts are vehemently expressed; tricks and cheatings are implied or insinuated and one cannot believe in it (whatever believing may mean in this context). This attitude pops up wherever something shows a divergence of or stands in contradicting to the general consensus. This includes simple esoteric topics as well as thousand-year old knowledge and traditions: for example, astrology, dowsing, acupuncture, the influence of the moon, the theory of signatures etc. All of it is not proved yet!

The whole thing would not be quite so bad, if this attitude was not accompanied by a real delusion and a need to persecute and annihilate. The otherness must be fought against and exposed. One must prove at all cost that one is right and the other one is wrong. Why not let people and things just be the way they are, whether one can grasp it or not? I have mentioned, how I was not interested in breatharianism over several years. It was nothing for me, but I was not really against it. I simply was not in resonance with it yet.

To conclude this part, I would like to quote from"

Der sechste Sinn und seine Phänomene". "The 6th sense and its phenomenons" by Dipl. Ing. Reiner Gebbensleben. On over 672 pages he describes innumerable experiments which prove and explain the phenomenon of the dowsing-rod. Not necessarily the book to go to sleep with. I admire this scientist for his courage, his deep intelligence and his mind-blowing testing capacities.

"Reducing research tests to standard elementary parts and considering them solely from the point of view of a uniquely specialized field does not lead either to real progress nor to the understanding of this complex system." (in this case radiesthesia)

I go on living fulfilled and in a pranic way. I live my daily life quite normally without the need to prove whatever, to convince whoever or to succeed in whatever tests.

PART 3: SURROUNDING THEMES

In this third part, I have gathered topics which recurrently cropped up during the P.P., which I had to particularly pay attention to or which seemed to be lacking or be misunderstood in the awareness of the people who I encountered in this phase, but also in human consciousness at large today like for example: What is Light?

1. MY MOTIVATIONS

My first and profoundest motivation for changing over to breatharianism is a spiritual motivation. My perception, my daily work with the aura, my metaphysical knowledge and the discoveries of modern physics confirm the subtle components as well as the Light components of humans. Photons and their emanations have been scientifically measurable for a few decades now. The human being originates from the subtle dimensions, the realms of spirit in which his soul's journey is anchored and to which he returns when he leaves his material vehicle at the end of his incarnation. His physical body is animated by the fire of life and kept alive by the very life impulse which is part of the all permeating and sustaining energy of the universe. Moreover, this force is boundless and eternal and is also called Light. Indeed, it livens up every atom of our being-ness – and of the rest of the creation. If this energy is present everywhere, therefore also in me, it should be possible to gain access to it and to nourish myself from it, shouldn't it? If these assumptions seem logical to you, may I invite you one step further? As this energy gives life and keeps each organ alive, each body system and each body tissue, why should it not be possible to swap over from material, solid food to pure energy as a nourishment?

I hope the mind of the reader, his right brain, his understanding and his need to grasp the topic is being somewhat contented now and should be allowed to rest. More information will be provided in the paragraph with the heading "What is pranic nourishment?"

Of course, psychological interest and readiness are the basis. At the beginning of the 1990´s, as I first heard of Breatharianism, I thought: Oh, that´s interesting, but I don´t understand why I should want to get my nourishment from Light. And so, I just brushed this topic aside. But a decade later it started cropping up in my mind, spontaneously, regularly and without any outer trigger. Time and time again it would come into my mind, but I did not want to consider it and I readily made up excuses:" It must be very difficult, and I can´t do it anyway". "I work a lot and never would have the time to make the P.P.". And once more I managed to put the prana issue aside. For a while at least. Until it came to my mind again. So it remained at the back of my mind until it slowly but decisively made its way into my consciousness. Anyway, I had the knowledge that human beings come from the Light realms and – being made of the Light – they are able to sustain themselves by the Light.

At that time, I gathered various observations. My digestive system could not deal with any excess or artificial additives anymore. Too much food eaten too late or even too quickly caused all kinds of discomfort. Foodstuffs with color additives, gluten, white sugar or even undeclared or unlisted toxins provoked unpleasant reactions. Besides, my body could distinguish whether the food had been handled with care and love or not, or even if it had been prepared a day or more ahead and therefore was not fresh. It was as if I had a detector in my stomach telling me when food was not pure or lifeless. My clairvoyance also discriminates between food that is alive and lightful or just filling material that has no life and at best fills up the stomach.

Gradually, I reduced my meals to a few live foodstuffs in organic quality, that means, food that provides the body and the whole being with life force. It is mainly raw. Moreover, I found out that too many ingredients thrown together actually produce an information chaos in the organism, which requires time and effort to unravel and eventually digest. These processes do not only rob a lot of intellectual, mental and inspirational potential, but on the physical level, the digestion of unbalanced meals take away attention and concentration, as one can often notice after lunch.

Then there was another observation many years ago. I was at the zoo where I kept seeing people constantly eating, chewing, biting and sucking; be it ice-cream, cigarettes, chewing gum, sandwiches, fruit, sweets, a proper meal or a snack. Of course, they also drank tea, coffee, water, soft drinks of all kinds. And this for hours on end. The oral phase à la Freud! You could well reproach me for going to the zoo in order to observe people. Actually, this is a justified reproach. My self-observation also unraveled a tendency to simply put something into my mouth, occasionally, thoughtlessly, just a little something to eat or drink – without hunger or thirst. Where does this obsession with swallowing things come from? Does the adult who is sitting at the computer all day really need three meals a day, probably something sweet in between, a bit of caffeine here and there and of course alcohol in the evening to make the whole thing bearable? Who on earth is able to consume that much anyway? Only the people in the industrialized countries, the ones who can afford it. And only over the last 50 years. For the rest of the world population it is not so obvious. And for a huge proportion of it, virtually unavailable.

As I already mentioned, already in my childhood and youth quite a few things seemed dubious to me, in particular this addiction to consumption which looks like a recurring litany of eating, sleeping, working. There is hardly any power, strength and time left for more. Nevertheless, I had to ground myself and I got caught up in these self-repeating cycles, like everybody else. At a certain point I decided that I was sufficiently anchored and tried to escape from these unceasing repetitions, which hold humans in the grip of the three lower chakras.

In the context of these observations I came to certain conclusions about nutritional habits and the effective nutritive value of foodstuffs. The close cooperation and machinations between agricultural economy, food industry and pharmaceutical industry is particularly remarkable. It makes sense to question the origin and the production of products and medicines and to thoroughly inform oneself. A lot of journalists, producers and researchers share their investigations with the public and even run great risks by doing so. The data, the numbers, the evidence are available to each and every one who cares for his dignity as a human being. And maybe also the dignity of the animal, the vegetable or the fruit which she/he is consuming. If the saying "You are what you eat" is right, one may estimate one's own worth/value sufficiently high as to demand solely fresh, raw and energy spending food. And should health be indeed our highest good, then we have deserved something better than the antibiotics, the pain killers and the hormones that are contained within the flesh of the animals as well as the fertilizers and herbicides etc. in the vegetables.

For the last several years I have been dedicating my life to what is alive and living and I connect myself to all that provides and generates sense, luminescence, optimism, trust and confidence. I am able to perceive energy, to measure energy and, as a medium, to ask questions. Consequently, I have already renounced a whole list of objects like TV, a fridge etc. In many own domains I have given up a whole lot of meaningless, time wasting actions and thinking habits.

My second motivation is a political one. It is a conscious decision to restrain my consuming attitudes/habits of consumption and to renounce/replace ill-making foodstuffs with prana nourishment. This way I am tapping into the highest source of nutrients. Human beings have a free will. We have choices. Actually, each minute demands a decision from us. Let us indeed make use of it! Each decision as well as each non-decision holds in itself certain consequences. I have taken the decision to dedicate my awareness, my attention, my intelligence, my ability to discriminate, the power of my thoughts, my love, my time, my strength and my force, my money, in a word my entire energy to authenticity and aliveness. Hence a peaceful resistance to stupidity, empty food, poisons and further degenerated products and habits takes place. This also includes a healthy manner of withdrawing one's own valuable energy from anything that is not worth it. No waffling about, no consuming, no waste of time and space. The natural consequence is a withdrawal from negative situations, ways of thinking, systems and useless and low-quality products. No energy, no resonance, no power put into them. In this context I go along with the pranic Afro American athlete Genesis Sunfire. He is one of the rare pranic people who implies a political aspect in his breatharian transformation. But also, Jasmuheen is hedging high ideals for humanity. She is promoting pranic nourishment as a solution to the narrow food supplies of the world population

As far as I am concerned, my motives are much more modest. I steadfastly practice what I consider to be right for myself. I do not see pranic nourishment as a solution or an opportunity for everybody. It was not always adequate for me either. But now it is exactly the appropriate mode of life for me.

I am always keen on making experiments and trying new things, for, although I enjoy reading and benefiting from the experience of other people, it is indispensable for me to gather my personal experiences. Above everything else I lead my life consistently and coherently in accordance with my credo.

2. MY PREPARATIONS

In the previous chapter I explained that my body has developed a more and more acute sensibility towards food that is not alive and loaded with poisonous additives. But even earlier I had a certain consciousness for natural and fresh food from bio-dynamic origin. Also, I was acquainted with vegetarianism, veganism as well as with the Bircher-Benner diet and philosophy.

I have to restrain/suppress a smile as I think of my mother, who already warned us back in the 60´s not to eat too much meat. And if we did, then only good meat from the farm. In any case, we should definitely avoid "hormone chickens" as she called them. Every day she prepared fresh vegetables from the garden. Later, as I worked in the Bircher-Benner naturopathic clinic, I ate my Bircher muesli every day (no finished dried products out of the plastic packet, but hand-made from freshly prepared ingredients). Also, I have already mentioned that I can see the frequency of foodstuff. It does not mean that I have always and solely eaten the right thing. I have also known greediness and stomach-cramps from eating too much food, bad food or stuff all thrown together. But regularly my body would let me feel the limits. Nowadays, I am grateful for it. This is my background.

Besides, my spiritual passion is ever growing, but its call is getting more and more urgent and cannot be ignored. Spirituality fills up my daily life. I cannot talk about it or teach it without living it fervently. I am one with my soul and follow my subtle perception and inner voice completely, particularly when they are so clear and precise.

Physical, emotional and mental cleansing, purification-rituals, phases of withdrawal, meditation and contemplation have long been part of my spiritual practice together with various forms of fasting. For short or rather long periods. Therefore, I know how my body reacts when detoxifying. In the last few years I limited myself to monodiets, because I had too little time for a complete fasting period. That way you eat one unique foodstuff all day for a week, e.g. only potatoes, rice or fruit. But this method was not satisfactory for me anymore. My system was in need of a more thorough cleansing and of a connection to a higher nurturing source.

I carried this thought around with me for a whole year. I never found the time for it. Too much work. Too little money to take a break. Invitations, travels, difficult projects. Feeling hungry. Fatigue. Well, a thousand excuses. But I used to think of the times when I was light and flexible. Ok, now I am 30 years older.

At last, I managed to fast again. I did not feel well. I looked bad. I had to realize how much I was polluted. I came to the conclusion that my spiritual consciousness was restricted and interfered with by my body which was full of impurities.

Then the big cleaning was due. After that I really felt better than before. I wanted to avoid falling back into the previous state. So I had to adopt better habits. Consequently, I felt lighter, more awake and clearer. From there onwards I did not only want to maintain this condition, but I wanted to optimize it. Regular physical exercise was added, which made me happy and contributed to my well-being, even if the beginning was marked by efforts, discipline and a lot of will power.

Spiritually my yearning grew all the more. I received the inspiration very clearly: it was time for pranic nourishment. I was interested, but putting it into praxis seemed far away and I doubted whether I was able to do it. Too difficult. Especially, if one leads a normal life. A lot of work. If one has to be very flexible in time and space. (I travel a lot and work very irregularly).

Parallel to this my body became more differentiating as far as food was concerned, especially through an experience I had on a holiday spent with an acquaintance abroad. There they served a buffet offering a huge variety of dishes which were wonderfully prepared. My acquaintance piled up a great deal of it on her plate, and got more of it a second and a third time. Everybody did it. And so did I. Until I started to feel bad. I reflected about it. Why such greediness? My acquaintance suffered from overweight and had stiff joints, although she was quite a bit younger than me. She attempted to do something good for herself by eating a lot. She was feeling an emptiness inside, which she tried to compensate with food. But deep within there was a profound self-rejection and even self-hatred. That was an important insight for me: Whenever I respect myself, I choose my food according to the requirements of my mind, my body and my daily functioning, which means I choose quality as well as in quantity.

Then my eating habits changed little by little. The amount got less, hence the real nurturing value got higher and higher.

I went on reading Jasmuheen's books which describe the spiritual connection to the ascended masters. Over the years, I had gathered some knowledge through my studies of theosophy and through my correspondence-courses at the Arcane School in London, where the works of Alice Bailey were/are thoroughly taught. Also, Vicky Wall rendered the approach to the masters easier to the public through the quintessences of Aura Soma. I studied several years with her and was one of the first people teaching Aura Soma, which I continued for several years. Personally, I have mixed feelings towards the masters. My perspective assumes that the Divine manifests itself through everything, also in human beings. The divine force and power should basically be accessible to all. What do we need masters for? Why should human beings eternally consider themselves as incomplete servants of earthly and heavenly masters?

I put this reflection aside and started the P.P. according to Jasmuheen between Christmas and the end of 2014. This period is energetically very charged through the winter solstice that contains the Light in its most secret essence. I exactly followed the instructions and stopped eating and drinking. And I waited. From time to time I communicated with the masters. I felt cold and lonely. I could see everything in me and in my life that was not in order. Then the detoxification started. Nothing new. I prayed. However, my spiritual attitude was as unstable as my physical reactions which got more and more unbearable. My aura was not particularly infused with Light because all doubts, fears and organic eliminations were gathering in there. My organism could not tolerate the fruit-juices one should at some time start drinking, and my blood pressure was very low. On the 19th day I was a pitiful appearance, and my process had nothing to do with Light. I came to the conclusion that I had done everything I should not do. Among other things, I had an unprepared start, I was leaving out fluids, and I was lacking the conviction that there was spiritual support. This experiment was a perfect success as far as I faced everything that was not in resonance with me and not in alignment with the Highest in an undistorted manner. Well, now I could work out what was right and meaningful. I was determined to take as long as I needed to be certain that I was really ready.

The next two years of preparation start with reading again. In this context I wish to thank Mr. Michael Werner whose book and further experiences impressed me a great deal. He is a doctor of chemistry and Anthroposophist.

Of all the literature about prana which I studied his report was the most valuable and decisive for me.

During the next two years I prepare my body in the direction of a less and better nourishment. I feel very good with a raw and fresh diet, and even better with smoothies made of organic fruit, herbs from my garden and self-germinated grains. I allow myself a gradual change over without dogmatism or stubbornness. On the contrary, nothing is forbidden, and I should enjoy what I eat. I can leave out what is not good for me without missing it. I deserve the best food that is good for my body and that gives me energy. Except for a few exceptions (either for cravings or because of lack of time) my menu indeed consists mainly of tasty smoothies. I am slowly losing weight and feel all the better for it.

Through literature and further information in the internet I discover many variations of P.P. or the change-over to pranic nourishment. Honestly, some of the offers seem completely unrealistic to me, others sound like a short fasting with guided meditations and affirmations. Some of them look like an experiment in converting one diet into another. Others again appear to be imagination-exercises paired with breathing technics. Like everywhere else it is necessary to first clarify one's own expectations and demands. And to make use of one's own ability to differentiate. For me it is clear: In less than 21 days I am not able to find the right approach to prana and anchor it in the cells.

So I have to plan for three weeks during which I shall not be travelling or teaching. A period in the middle of the winter is not favorable because of the cold. The energies of the spring are fresh and invigorating like the juices that flow through the veins of nature. Or maybe the crop of the autumn, I wonder. At best, it must be in the summertime with the warmth of the sun, the tendency to extraversion, the period when one can be outside in the nature, the season when I physically feel the fittest. I leave the precise time open and focus on my state of mind and my present condition. Such a process should take place when you feel well in every respect: health, finances, relationships. Nothing should be nagging at one's general condition or weaken the immunity system or activate chronic problems or should eventually divert or deter me from the process. No moving out, no divorce and no wedding either. To my way of thinking the phase of transformation and the installation of prana in the auric field and in the cells is a very special period of time which should be paramount to everything else. For me it gradually became clear, that, if I managed this metamorphosis, then I would be aiming at definitely adopting the pranic way of life. The three weeks are not a test to see whether it is possible. Many people have already done it. I have already gone through fasting phases lasting three weeks and more. As a matter of fact, I only want to become and remain pranic. That´s it – if I only manage the change-over.

Little by little I prepare my body by drinking smaller smoothies. I also I also experiment with food-supplements. I want to ensure that I start the process with everything I need and do not suffer from weakness or lack of nutrients. In my head I have already renounced shopping, cooking, washing up etc. a long time ago!

Also my spiritual state is changing. I am longing for long meditations. The connection the higher world or rather within is starkly growing. I really miss it when I neglect it because of lack of time. My inner communication is getting more precise. My approach to the Light has constantly been accompanying me and carrying me in my evolution. I perceive it and use it in my work. Light and love are the two sides of the same unity. The clarity of Light and its clearing proprieties are primordial for me in this incarnation as opposed to previous lives, when the ability to give and to receive love was essential. The Light is my raison d´être, simultaneously my deepest longing and my deepest fulfillment. Light as nourishment?

I am looking forward to the P.P. Nevertheless, I perceive a slight uncertainty. The project needs to be anchored through practical reflections and decisions. When does it start, when does it end, which persons will accompany me? Which practical preparations do I have to care for? (Dear Gitta faithful and trustful is always available during important changes) I want to decide on a relatively close point in time, otherwise enthusiasm and drive may start waning. One more condition is getting clear: I shall do the process alone and not in a group. As I committed several mistakes two years ago, I now know what to avoid! And my ego is not so overwhelming that it would not comply: Should I feel unwell, either physically or mentally, I would interrupt the experiment or event end it.

So I decided to do the three week P.P. during the Easter holidays. On 11th April 2017 I begin my new life.

3. MY PHYSICAL METAMORPHOSIS
a) During the process
The switch over to pranic nourishment and to the installation of the Light within the ether-body and the cells takes place in three weeks. You have participated in this process through my report.

What happened during this time? Physical cleansing and elimination take place. They are – at least at the beginning of the process – similar to a fasting phase. That is the reason why one should have previously experienced one´s own body while fasting. As a part of it there are usual and normal symptoms, nevertheless I emphasize the personal and individual consequences. They are dependent upon various factors, for example personal sensations, the subjective self-observation and how heavily the body tissues are polluted. For somebody a headache may be easily bearable, particularly when one knows that it is caused by the elimination process and will only last for a short time. Someone else may feel ill right from the beginning. The individual perception of discomfort obviously correlates with the contact to one's own body. It is advisable to develop a healthy and especially trustworthy relationship to one´s own physicality before starting the P.P. because its cells are telepathic.

I have experienced relatively few elimination symptoms, because my system was already cleared by the long preparation and the previous conversion to a diet of smoothies. Light headache, a coated tongue and stiff articulations for a couple of hours, that was all. The circulation suffered most during the process.

During the 21 day process the bowels are still active. Among other things it is important to take in a lot of fluids during this phase so as to flush out the cells, the intestines and other body systems. Towards the end of the week there is a strong emptying of the bowels, as if the body would understand and say: Now I am getting rid of everything and I make tabula rasa! It is all the more astonishing, because there is no food intake, apart from herbal teas and water.

At the beginning skin and complexion do not look particularly beautiful, for they are eliminating. As I spend a lot of time outside, I rapidly become sun-tanned, which lends me at least a healthy look. But relatively quickly there is a visibly positive change in the skin. It improves step by step, and the old spots disappear gradually. The dry skin on my feet, which has needed good care in the last few years, spontaneously gets soft and young again, although I am still walking barefoot in the garden.

Many pranic people report a weight loss at the beginning. By far not all of them. For me loss of fat is nearly problematic. Or, in other words: I am making a little problem out of it. I rapidly lose a lot of weight, which is rather disadvantageous for me being small. I had already lost weight before the process and I do not have much reserve. It is a good idea to start the process with a few extra kilos. The further loss of weight – after the 21 days – draws my attention. Less physical mass leads to a physical and an energetic instability I feel too light, have no grounding and find it difficult to walk straight. I would love to put a couple of stones in each pocket to recover my stability. As a matter of fact, other people have even more worries than me about their weight. All they see is the weight loss, although there would be a few other things to notice. There exists a real fixation on the weight in this society.

I usually have a good sleep. But the quality of the pranic sleep surpasses all expectations and hopes. It is exceptionally regenerative and refreshing, comparable with the sleep of childhood: deep and free of worries. And its duration is half as long. In my case, sleep duration did not necessarily get reduced to half, as it is often described. Even as a pranic woman I remain a rather long sleeper. Maybe, because I appreciate sleep so much. I still need four to five hours sleep.

As soon as the elimination period is over, I develop a great deal of physical strength and resistance. I also have a higher pain tolerance. I have an incredible drive at my disposal, and I get up at four in the morning with an incomparable enthusiasm and walk for hours in the park and along the river Isar. This recovering of mobility and this rejuvenation remind me of my childhood, even if the skin is not so nice at specific places now, due to the loss of weight. I can only wonder at my delight at/in movement and at the stamina of the body. I cannot remember having read about the advantages of pranic sleep. I have a greatly increased kinetic energy at my disposal. This is a pleasant surprise for me.

The only consequence of the installation of prana that I do not appreciate is the sensitivity to the cold due to fat reduction. I beg your pardon for the repetitions pertaining to my new sensation of coldness (I have even cancelled quite a few), but it affects my present condition on several levels. I was expecting spring temperatures and spring feelings, but it snowed at Easter. In the flat the heating was on quite high, which is unusual for me. I put on many layers of clothing and for the first time in my life I wore long underpants. Good that I got rid of that weight burden: now there is plenty of space for all the layers. Later I escaped from the cold to the Tessin.

Then comes summertime and the warmth is welcome and beneficial!

b) The processes within the process

My P.P. is further supported by an exceptionally favorable astrological constellation. The planet Mars is directly firing my Jupiter. Originally, I did not know anything about it. I hear about this support by chance as I have a conversation with an astrologer. Naturally, this constellation lends me a lot of strength and is almost a warranty that the P.P. will be successful.

Even when the pranic modus is already installed, the process goes on. From my point of view the metamorphosis goes on: a certain stage has been attained, but the elimination goes on in a slower manner. Rather cyclic I would claim. Organs or systems which have shown a weakness before the BP may bring new symptoms. My perception tells me that the cleaning of the body, the cleansing of the tissues and the clearing of the plasma will continue for a while still. I have lived on solid food for 63 years. That leaves traces in the organism. The body has a certain set of rules that are governed by Saturn, and they require time to integrate all that is new. Nevertheless a few more reactions are awaiting the nurse, the therapist and the woman with fasting background. Definitely not as acute as during the 21 day change over, but the cleansing goes on. Indeed, I have some discomfort with my digestive system. Nothing new, but really concentrated as I have not experienced it for decades, because I lived healthily and avoided everything that was not digestible.

Also, after the process my weight reaches a point at which I have to be attentive. The symptoms are unpleasant, when the system is taking the fat from the organs. It is painful and dangerous. And with sunken in cheeks I look bad. I have the impression that the mass is missing, and I find it difficult to remain in the body. It may be that my fat-metabolism is hyperactive. On these days I take in a little honey, the crystallized kind, because it is naturally pure. If necessary, also a little organic fluid cream, which I can well assimilate, for it does not get registered as animal protein by the body. Already in the past I had good results with it. However, my body cannot get on with oils, even the finest like for example linseed oil. Of course I am acquainted with Dr. Budwig's wonderful diet and all the recommendations of vegan people. But my body provides me with the adequate scale or criteria through its changing reactions and the language of its cells and organs, independent of all those good advices. As time goes by the weight has been stabilizing itself for several weeks. I am feeling well in this light body, as I had known it all the years, until the menopause. It also tallies with the body-shape which I and my younger sister have inherited from our mother. This figure is the one that lies in the genes. My system has let go of the burden, the unnecessary weight, which is beneficial for the articulations, the skin, the blood circulation etc.

The fixation on eating seems to be inseparable from the fixation on weight. Two sides of the same coin, I suppose. I came to the conclusion that my loss of weight is more of a problem for certain people around me than for myself. My body is well trained. As time goes by, the overactive phase wanes will calm down. I don't have the time to do mountain tours anymore. And the influence of Mars is now over.

I have rarely weighed myself and then only at particular points in time. I want to distance myself from this "Measure everything!", "Weigh everything!", from this compulsive way of wanting to divide and control life only in measurable units instead of breathing in and out sheer aliveness in happy and confident gulps. I do not need to weigh myself; my body sends me the necessary messages. And my tightest pair of trousers, too! I do see how it droops. I have also noticed that variations in weight in the pranic state can be impressive and depend upon the balance of fluids within the body. It is not unusual that I lose one kilo over night without perspiring. In connection with this observation I have been wondering about the medical follow up and research concerning Dr. Michael Werner in Switzerland. There they determined that he had lost weight under 24 hours video-camera observation, although he has been living on pranic nourishment for years.

How is it possible to make a general and rigid model, to assess an organism which now basically functions in a modus that is entirely different from the usual criterion? This blinkered attitude has conquered the world and considers itself advanced, superior and all knowing. The results are sometimes absurd, sometimes even (self-)destructive.

I have integrated the pranic way of life into my daily life. The whole thing has become normal to me. I only talk about it when necessary. I enjoy going to coffee places and some restaurants with friends and acquaintances and sip at a cappuccino for a whole hour or more. I then recognize the smell and the taste of the coffee as something very special. My body reacts to these exceptions in very different manners. Sometimes I get diarrhea within two hours, another time a wonderful feeling spreads in my belly and I feel the effect of the coffee, after which I can also slide into a deep sleep without any problem. My reactions seem to have to do with the additives. But my body sometimes tolerates coffee which is not organic.

You will now think that I have plenty of time at my disposal, because I do not go shopping, do not cook and wash up anymore. It is only partly true. I need a lot of discipline, because I have many different interests and divide my life into various domains. I take time to care for my body, do my physical exercises and my meditations. Introducing an order or at least a new order in my surroundings, my projects and my plans, as well as maintaining this order, demands time and a focused will. I work a great deal also helping others without remuneration, for fulfillment and well-being want to be shared with others.

Please do not be envious: I can also get into a scrape and suddenly have to run not to miss the underground. The large amount of time which seemed available during the P.P. has now shrunk. I have to extend the factor time again and to adjust it to my present requirements, for time is elastic. The essential point concerning time is to be able to re-appropriate it to oneself by learning to spend time with activities that really matter. Anything else is really a waste...not only of time. „Who and what do I spend my time with, doing what and how?" is definitely an issue, also for non-pranics.

As time goes by the pranic sleep evolves slightly: in quality as well as in quantity. In the wintertime I need a little more sleep. It tends to be deeper and more oblivious than in summertime where it is lighter. Which quality is that? I easily fall asleep and wake up like a child. By waking up I very clearly feel how I reintegrate my physical body and I immediately want to undertake something. Also, I am immediately aware of where I am, and which tasks and appointments are expecting me today. This has not always been obvious in my case, for I travel a great deal and often wake up at different places. The sleep is deep and very regenerating. Sometimes I bring along some atmosphere or mood, a solution or an idea from beyond.

c) The pranic body

How different the pranic body is reacting can best be ascertained by observing its excretions, their smell and their color. The amount is less and lighter than with solid modes of nourishment. Also the perspiration and the body smell are more subdued. I do appreciate this, all the more, because the own senses have become finer and more developed. Following the phase of elimination, the urine is clear and thin and would be very appropriate for urine therapy, because the inhibitory factors are lowered if it hardly smells or tastes of urine but rather sweet and fruity.

A body that hardly smells anymore does not leave any odor of sweat on clothes, shoes, bedding and textiles with which it comes into contact. In spite of this I am very clean and hygienic – more so than before.

I care for my body with great precision. My body is trained and strong. I am healthier than before. I do not have any cravings. I enjoy smelling food or looking at appetizing plates without having the need to ingest it. It is all like a beautiful memory with all my former sensations. I can recall them up very precisely and leave them where they belong: in my memory.

In my mouth I always have various taste sensations but mainly those of saltiness and sweetness, which alternate or sometimes delightfully combine. Do you know those salty caramels from the Bretagne? Yes, you've got it, just the same as those (but without the calories). Now, I am tempting you! Sorry, I apologize! When I am not feeling well and I losing weight, I tend to get a rather bitter taste in my mouth. A whole lot of chemical processes are still taking place in this body. I am not solely constituted of Light yet, and some transformations can be perceived through the prevailing taste in the mouth.

d) The rhythms and my idiosyncrasies

During the change-over and the anchoring of the prana I often reflected about my reactions. I did have certain expectations that the process would follow a straight line. This attitude was based on the literature which I had read and the comments of some people who occasionally assisted me. When I read a report, I am the receptionist of an overview and a résumé of events and experiences. While I am immersed in it every second, my perspective is more emotional and chaotic. I sometimes experience various streams of feelings and felt sense moods simultaneously; and they originate and cover various aspects; sometimes they even leave the impression of contradicting each other. The different facets of my being are confronted by inner pictures, which are at times overwhelming. I can be in heaven through the essence of the last meditation and at the same time depressed by the appearance of my body, that has lost too much weight; and in addition to that I can be worried that I keep on getting thinner and that some of my dear friends cannot understand, why I chose a pranic life. Then, again the sun shines and I enjoy the warmth so intensely, that I get into an ecstatic state. The experiencing is highly concentrated. I am on top of the world at this moment. It is, as if my whole life has been yearning for this pranic state. But on the 21st day I am down. I am unable to rejoice. Not even a, "Hi, I've made it!" I know, I do not want to nourish myself either vegan or vegetarian, even less by consuming meat. But pranic? Not really, either. What then, now? Meditation restores my inner balance.

Now, I have told this all to show there are ups and downs during the process and beyond. Nevertheless, I have never doubted that the decision to follow this path was the right one for me.

Today I had a very enriching exchange. I am gaining an entirely different perspective: the process is a row of organic occurrences that unfold in waves. A rocking back and forth that would not be recognized for what it is, were it be looked upon as static and its rhythms ignored. A deep metamorphosis is taking place on several planes: however, not necessarily simultaneously. This means that some subtle layers absorb and integrate the prana more or less readily than others, although the process mainly happens in the prana- or ether-body. In addition to the regular cycles there are periodic cycles overlapping a particular phase: all is well, but then, in my case, I have to adjust the situation to the present feedback of the body losing weight, for example.

On can see that this applies to many pranic persons. Only few of them manage to give up food and drink all at once and constantly. Also the pranics who are now only drinking a few sips of water a week, even they have known a progressive reduction over time. At the beginning they needed more fluids or sleep. An evolution was taking place. The straight development which our left hemisphere would like to see is rather contrary to prana, which IS life and the life force. The quality of life is change, unfolding in waves and cycles. It makes sense to me to regard the P.P. and the following time in this Light and to flow with it instead of fighting the actual situation. I find it interesting to communicate telepathically with my body and my cells. The fact is, that they are telepathic 24 hours a day and not only when I give a reasonable lecture: Now, dear cells, we only want to be 100% pranic until the end of this incarnation. It is indeed my intention. But my body might have other plans; it also listens to messages from the unconscious, which surface from the collective as well as from individual pools.

And now let us look at the pattern „Fear of losing weight". Originally, I wanted to work on it by the bias of hypnosis. A pretty trick for the left brain: something is disturbing its program. So the program should be switched off. The human person is a machine, a computer.

Something does not fit, and it gets switched off, so that it goes along with the general or agreed view. My perception is rather a natural, organic and vivid one. My conception of life is a feminine, mystical and flowing approach, which experiences the meanders of the moment in a flexible and supple manner. And now it is time for slowing down the pranic state by including the requirements of the physical body. In any case, I am keeping to fluids.

Rhythms, cycles and variations mark one's own life with ever changing phases: yes, pranic life is like "normal" life, at best embedded in a deep inner certainty with a healthy and ever growing distance to the transformations just described. Yes, I am full up; and being replete with Light expresses itself through a direct confidence in the rightness of the moment.

Together with the concept of "rhythms", I wish to consider the concept of ‚process'. This word reveals a development, a chronological succession of various events which either build upon one another or run into each other or move somehow backwards, forwards, up and down. In any case, something is happening: an evolution is taking place. This is the opposite of a static condition. The goal is not reached yet. Maybe it will never be reached, because „the way is the goal", as the Taoists say. And the way is here to be treaded, to be experienced with all cells, senses, feelings, reflections and insights which it may call forth. This is the opposite of a button which is pressed – and there, I have the supposed answer. Within the process there is no generally valid answer, but rather a row of experiences and ventures which have been lived through, which tally with the being who is treading the way, or not. I am still living in a pranic modus, because I experience an ever growing, unfolding agreement with my inner being. The day when the Light nourishment does not feel right anymore, I can decide to change over to another diet. It is so simple and so free. The pranic state entices one to be awake and demands flexibility, self-responsibility and clarity – also a good amount of introspection. This is how I once again stumbled over one of my particularities. It is not rare, in my case, that complications, variations or divergences appear in the development of things which would otherwise go smoothly and without problems for most people. Somehow, I have something that predestines me to this; although, or maybe because I always do things as they should be done, maybe even a little too precise. Anyway, I always manage to experience things even more thoroughly by the bias of exceptions or special situations of which nobody else would dream of. This disposition for divergences and specialties has a big advantage: I gather so many experiences and win insights into backgrounds and alternatives, that I can see through much that may seem obvious at first sight. However, I can win a deeper understanding of occurrences that would not reveal everything they hold, would they have gone smoothly. For me, as a teacher in naturopathic schools, this is a huge treasure of knowledge and direct experiencing, also, as far as mistakes and side aspects are concerned. Such experiences allow me to discover and research links and connections which are rarely mentioned, or ways of behaving that should definitely be avoided – and all of this firsthand and fundamentally. This enriches my teaching, and I can go into the reasons, whys and hows and tell a few tales – all first-hand!

That way I have reached the conclusion that each P.P. is an individual metamorphosis. Prana nourishment is not the same as prana nourishment. Each pranic person brings her/his quite personal disposition into the process. For me it is important to define clearly how I experience the living on Light, what it means for me and how I want to go on living with it. This is why this definition and the experiences associated with it are solely valid for me. Here it is all about my change over to prana nourishment. And I am pranic in my own personal way, in my own rhythm and with all idiosyncrasies which belong to me.

4. MY STATE OF MIND

I predominantly feel well throughout the process, optimistic and confident, except on the 21st day when I am not really able to enjoy my success.

I also mentioned that I experienced certain emotional fluctuations. To be more precise, these refer to various layers of emotional sensations, which I experience simultaneously. At times, them being opposite to each other generates an inner splitting. "Am I happy?" I sometimes ask myself during the process. "Yes", answers a deeply moving recognition, which nearly brings tears to my eyes. But in the next moment I am completely dismayed, because the DHL messenger rings at the door and tears me away from my ecstasy. As I open the door, I do not show my reaction, of course, but I thank him for delivering the packet.

Enthusiasm is nothing new for me as a Sagittarian woman. But the pranic state has definitely intensified it. Beauty and harmony or simply well-cut hair or pleasant and respectful exchanges with people fill me with delight. The right timing of the moment always surprises and delights me. This feeling-thinking also remains when the more emotional overtones have dissipated. Gradually, the fluctuations and oscillations find a balance and I gain more distance to my emotional body as time goes by.

During the process I feel rather permeable, and external fears and projections are particularly unpleasant for me. I require better boundaries. Sleeping in dormitories is definitely not possible for me anymore. I am also receptive for other people's reactions while asleep.

The perception of the senses and the mind is not only more intensive, it also penetrates into greater depths, but at the same time it is getting more resistant. It is not so that an oversensitivity as the result of an overwhelming receptivity or an exaggerated emotionality or vulnerability is present, as is the case when the aura layers are communicating in a disharmonious manner between each other. In such a state there is disarray between feeling and thinking. Ether, astral and mental bodies are not in resonance. Which is not the case within the pranic mode.

Through the change-over I have become more spontaneous, clearer, but not necessarily more diplomatic. I see a few things ahead of time. They are already quite obvious before they take place. I cannot bear too much closeness and especially not for a long time. I need more space to myself, for my aura is wider. I believe I have gained a better overview of my own processes but also of outer developments pertaining to me as well as to other persons. I am less "stuck" in it, but at the same time my approach is more empathic and understanding.

My love of tidiness and order has become conspicuous, not that I used to be untidy, but it has gained proportions which cannot be overlooked. Indeed, it happened in the past that I would not wear a piece of clothing because I did not get around to sewing a button on it or doing some small repair. Now there are no such unfinished or incomplete little jobs. And what is particularly gratifying is that I manage them all. My hair lies properly, I can arrange the flowers in the vase as I wish, and the little sewing job can be done without first losing the needle or having to untangle the thread before I start. The pranic transformation has thrown Light upon my approach to the material world. Strange, isn´t it? Most things in my life are flowing in the right order. I recognize the appropriateness of things, and my ego can accept them as well. This generates an inner peace. The concept of "with ease" comes to my mind, simple and light, without effort. To be in the flow. Moreover, "ease" is the opposite of "disease".

As soon as the prana was installed, I got the message that feeding on Light is only a springboard for me and that it is no end in itself. It means I have passed an examination, but the next one is already waiting for me. One step after another. And I shall discover where the path is leading. Just like in real life

5. MY SPIRITUAL TRANSFORMATION
a) Self-esteem and food

The choice to nourish myself is one of the most important decisions of my life. I have invested enough time and reflection into this project and not only in the last two years with the gradual change of diet. It was crystal clear to me that this decision should only originate from my Higher Instance, from my utter sovereignty, and not out of my ego, as a passing mood or out of curiosity, and not under the influence of people around me. It is worth following an authentic and pure motivation in all matters anyway. I would never encourage or try to convince anybody to do the P.P. or even make an attempt. It comes from within and one knows exactly that it is the right option. Anything that has to do with simple curiosity or having a try for adventure´s sake should be recognized as such: it is a game, an excitement for the bored Westener. Ok, nothing against it. But please, be honest (yes, with yourself, who else?) and first start with short fasting periods under proper professional guidance.

The saying "You are what you eat" makes sense as far as it is a mirror of the self-esteem and the awareness of a person. What we feed our cells on influences our thoughts, our feeling-thinking and our behavior.

I am not judging or condemning any kind of foodstuff or any diet. But please, be aware of what is adequate for you at the moment, by whom and how your food was killed and which toxins it contains! The chemical reactions naturally occurring within the body definitely have a determining influence on the thinking process and the behavior.

Even the way I reacted to smoothies was impressive. The feeding on Light is an even more far-reaching experience, that impregnates the whole life and leads to more self-responsibility and to a more consequent manner of being and acting. I am more myself. The clearing which is taking place as well within and without renders everything transparent and authentic. And what still requires cleaning will attract the spotlight of attention until it is dealt with.

In the last few months, I have developed new manners of working and discovering a lot of new things. That can help people spiritually, energetically and on the subtle planes. In a

way I have become more intelligent, more empathic, but I am entirely allergic to silliness and overweening sentimentality. It is time for humanity to become adult.

b) My spiritual connection

The spiritual connection is an indispensable prerequisite. It has nothing to do with churches or religious institutions. It is a natural connection to "All That Is" and to the awareness of the Eternity, in which all cells are bathing. This connection is available to each and every one, anytime and anywhere. And it is free.

I am bathing in it. It is guiding me, it heals, nourishes and protects me. It expresses itself through guidance and intuition, through the inner dialog with pictures and feelings, through the asking and receiving, what is available for me.

The intensity of my spiritual

connection increased all along the P.P. It became stronger, clearer and more intensive. It provides my life flow with trust and a flexible intuition, adapted to all situations.

Grace accompanies and follows the meanders of transmutation and transformation, for there are changes occurring on one side in the way of thinking (mental) and on the other side in the form (the physical body).

Parallel to this, the readiness to take responsibility for myself as spirit, soul and body, as well as for all actions and non-actions is indispensable. The capacity to take spontaneous decisions also – as in the case where I would decide to change my mind and put an end to my breatharian diet.

The spiritual connection is a confirmation of self-sufficiency, balance and of having enough. What results from this insight is a simple life with needs which are always richly fulfilled: one always gets what one needs. No more, no less. And the inspiration, the guidance and the synchronicities crop up – unexpectedly in alignment with the Highest Good, when one has clearly expressed what is required. The spiritual links, the Light are the opposites of precarity, grabbing and blind materialism.

Here is a concrete example for it: I have mentioned that I have been benefitting from a very favorable astrological constellation during the whole of the P.P. I had no idea about it as I took the decision of doing the change -over during the period from 11. 04 till 01.05.2017. Actually, I had other practical criteria in sight pertaining to my teaching work. I found Easter energetically interesting. I know that I am rather good at choosing the right time set-up, simply out of my life experience. But the fact that I would precisely choose this exceptionally favourable phase, which only happens once in twelve years, can only be a sign of a clear guidance. Indeed, the planet Mars provided me with a great deal of force, endurance, resistance and fighting spirit.

I have decided to go through the P.P. alone – not in a group – in a very reflected manner. The reason for it, is that I wanted to receive the guidance and the instructions only from my Higher Self. The serenity and the reclusion without distraction were particularly important to me.

Maybe still a word to discipline. A couple of times I was told: "Oh yes, I could do it also for I have a lot of discipline" or the opposite:" I would never have the discipline for it!"

I have asked myself how much discipline I really have. Do I have endurance? Of course, when we take a concrete decision, it is necessary to exercise focus, determination and will. Actually, it is less a matter of discipline. It is rather the dedication to a higher purpose which motivates me. In any case prana nourishment should not be a kind of self-inflicted torment It would then be contrary to the freedom of self-determination with the inner agreement.

c) Meditation

I obtained the original meditation from a person who has been pranic for a long time. I have altered it gradually, according to my requirements and my guidance. The meditation is important and life giving, like nectar. It is the place where I recharge my batteries, my connection to the source. I practice it regularly. Here it makes sense to emphasize that we are always and constantly spiritual beings, not only when we are meditating or trying to be or look holy. The splitting between spiritual and material - in the West as well as in the East - leads to a distortion of truth, to power games and manipulation. The fact is, that there would be no physical body, no cells and whatever, if there were no subtle levels, no Light, which would inform the body or define a cell as a liver-cell. Whether somebody is interested in spiritual topics or ways of life in general right now, is a matter of development. We are free to decide, whether spirituality is now of interest for us or not. Each being is part of the all-encompassing force.

This is the consciousness I focus on in my daily life. It is for me a lightful, life-accepting attitude, full of beauty and blissfulness.

The capacity of perception of the senses and of the higher senses, such as clairvoyance, clairaudience and clear knowledge is more pronounced since the conversion to prana. I have a quote for you from a book that I can dearly recommend: "Vitamine, Mineralstoffe, Spurelemente. Gesund und fit mit Vitalstoffen. Ein kritischer Ratgeber" by Heinz Knieriemen. Mr. Knieriemen does not only give numerous tips, information and valuable explanations in an easily understandable manner, he also owns a deeper knowledge about the true relationships and connections between the mind and the body reactions. Please read page 64 of his book. I share this quote with you to spare you the way:

"We are able to defend the peaceful and serene sensual delight against the universal craziness of fast life and fast food. And so we carry further the bacillus of sensual pleasure and we refuse to obey whenever the attainment of pleasure is in danger".

It lies in the perspective and the attitude, in the gratefulness and the enthusiasm about our natural creation, about the wonder of beingness in its entirety. This is meditation.

6. SUPPORT AND ACCOMPANIEMENT

a) Morphogenetic fields

The concept of fields made its appearance in the 30s of the 20th century in the domain of physics. I am thinking, for example, of Dr. Saxton Burr, who discovered the life-field per chance and who was followed by many other researchers who made use of this concept. Ruppert Sheldrake met with form-giving patterns, which represent intentions in their subtle form and gradually impregnate the structure of reality with the corresponding material level. What surrounds us is a construction which unfolds through time and recurrence, that is an expansion of mental forms or concepts in a concrete and experienced so-called reality. Sheldrake lends them the name of 'morphogenetic fields'.

As far as our theme is concerned it is the morphogenetic field of pranic nourishment; it is not yet anchored in the 3rd dimension, in which most of humanity finds itself. It is not yet part of people´s everyday life. Which factor would find an access into the brains of people in order to provide a space or a place in their minds? Precisely, the use of the concept, the recognition of its possibility and feasibility will establish its real value on the manifestation level. This is basically the story of the 100th monkey washing his potato or peeling his banana. And so, new habits, concepts or devices need their time until they find acceptance. Unfortunately, big parts of humanity lose themselves in the use of and dependency on electronics, which are robbing them of practicing their true capacities and keeping them from their genuine potential. All this in a nearly unnoticed manner.

Looking at it from a different angle: Each person who deals with the subject of pranic alimentation (or whatever new or forgotten concept), mentally, emotionally or through empirical experience, contributes to this topic. At the same time a reality bubble is created, which, like a pool or a reinforcing matrix, affects each and every one who is interested in it somehow. The progress, the recognition and experiences which I have gathered in this context are collected in this prana morphogenetic field, like the experiences of all other pranic people at all times and places. This collection forms again a reservoir, which tapped into as a strengthening mental and energetic field. It is also used with purpose and intent, when one connects to it through resonance and telepathy. This is what I consciously practice nearly every day. This is simultaneously my contribution and the advantage which I can draw from when I make myself receptive for the wisdom of other pranic people.

By the way, everything that we experience has a direct influence on this specific area and contributes to the communal pool of knowledge and experience of humanity. And, last but not least, it also serves the further development of the inhabitants of planet earth at large. Considering things from this perspective nobody is permitted to underestimate what she/he does or does not do, nor is he or she to undervalue their responsibility to the Whole. We are the cells of a huge organism, and each human being contributes to either the health or the sickness of this paramount being. And naturally, there exists a constant interaction and interdependence between the Whole and each single one of us. It is akin to the concept of the Akashic records.

b) Guidance from various planes

I benefit from the guidance of various spirit guides on this path. I divide them into the following categories:

My totem animals, also called power animals, are the wolf and the spider. They instruct me about my instinctive reactions and about the development of the process. They may appear either aggressive or supporting. In any case, they do not spare the human ego. They belong to the animal kingdom and definitely exhibit other qualities than the human ones. Their guidance is indispensable, for they are important helpers, if they agree to the process. That way a very intimate relationship can unfold.

The morphogenetic field of the pranic population is present everywhere in the world. This energetic entity contains the knowledge and the experiences of all pranic people who have ever been. The more recent tendencies in particular offer another approach, together with the new paradigms. Also informations pertaining to the spiritual traditions of the West or of the East are contained in this reservoir of knowledge, whether directly or indirectly linked to the breatharian process. This applies, for example, to Theresia Neumann or the Chi Gong masters, just to mention a couple of them. The scientific approach to the pranic themes is represented in this pool, for example, by the book and the reports of Dr. Michael Werner. The research of thousands of people, who are interested in pranism, and their readiness to experiment are also registered within that field, even if they have only been practicing for a short spell of time. Among others I am referring to participants of the 21-day-process who at the end of it return to solid nourishment. Their experiences are a valuable contribution to those who will be following their steps at a later date.

Moreover, I equally count the physical and material body as an entity that delivers feedbacks which cannot be overseen, and which are rich in consequences. In this quality the physical body takes a leading position.

The spirit guides respect our free will, but they also answer prayers and invocations. They make themselves noticeable through the higher senses like clairvoyance and clairaudience, if they are developed. Under certain circumstances, the guides might send signs through particular constellations of events, so as to point to the appropriate path or hinder a plan which might not be fruitful or even harmful. Synchronicities equally belong to the clues and references of daily reality, such as chance coincidence, hazard, inspiration, dreams, also our intuition, our gut-feelings as well as flashes and whole series of spontaneous reactions, which our intellect mostly does not register, but which lead and guide us, protect us and even save us.

Constantly and everywhere, we are embedded in and embraced by the powerful and loving intention of The Life. This understanding opens up the doors to the experience of spirit via the manifested plane.

c) Harmonious synchronicities

They fill up the flow of life with congruent events and they are the source of deep satisfaction. They express themselves through the fact that we are at the right time at the right place with the right people. Events unfold in a harmonious coherence, and I often get the impression that each action fits and that the guidance is present down to the simplest and most basic matters. Here is a little example: As I have lost quite a bit of weight, my underwear has become too large and uncomfortable. At some point in time I spontaneously received the idea that I should go to an outlet shop that I do not particularly like and where I had not yet found anything worthwhile. But on that day I found just the right thing: underwear of a very good Swiss manufacturer, which fit perfectly and is very pleasant to wear. And at a very good price!

Does this mean that the Light, my Higher Self, my guidance is interested in the wellness of my backside? I came to the conclusion that in a strange manner it is indeed the case, for everything is connected to everything else. The levels are tightly interwoven with each other. What is right above, should also be so below, and this also applies to the opposite direction.

The material plane, the "details", as I used to call them despitefully, have cost me sufficient frustration in this lifetime. In the last decades many things actually improved in my attitude and in my way of dealing with so called reality, with a tiny part of it: with the terrestrial art of daily life. I am well grounded; I have landed here after 40 or 50 years. Some need a little longer. The remembrance of other levels does not fade away so quickly for everybody.

In my pranic state I do not only get on better with the material world, but my consciousness, together with my inner guidance, is embracing it with reverence as a part of the divine. And it gets looked after and cared for. I used to think of myself as tidy and clean, but now it is a matter of taking care of the manifested world. Disorder hurts me and I cannot bear it very long. It is a feeling that permeates my whole being. I am not only upset or refuse to live in a disorderly place, but I am literally missing a harmony from which I now have more of an idea, or my cells have a better remembrance of it. Nowadays I pay attention and appreciate every detail. Each thing has its place and it is all about transferring this awareness in my daily life and in my surroundings. Beauty has become even more important.

Beauty means in its true sense: order, fairness or harmony, where each and everything occupies its place as a tiny part of the big puzzle, as belonging to the divine order. And in this divine order underwear should also fit properly.

With the conversion to prana I have gone through a transformation. My vibration is different. I notice that some things are not valid or appropriate anymore. Old things are getting replaced by new habits, new people and new products. I wish a different shampoo from the one I have been using for ages, and just now somebody offers me a wonderful hair-washing-cream. I need a new dentist, for the gentleman I have been going to for years is now underqualified for the treatment I need. And promptly I read about a lady dentist who works in a more holistic manner...

The interaction between awareness and manifesting reality flows effortlessly in the realm of reality. Many things are getting simpler, clearer. I enjoy the relationships between human beings, animals, the correspondence with places and spaces, opportunities and situations. Things originate "per chance" and fulfill the requirements and wishes of people in small as well as in large matters. Whoever remains awake and careful observes the workings of fate and divine providence, which are weaving reality out of the huge cosmic dance and mirroring the deepest yearnings. To achieve this, it is useful to let go of the madness of illusion and find an open door or even an inconspicuous crack, which no one has yet noticed...

Ease is the opposite of dis-ease.

d) Therapeutic help

I have an excellent osteopath who works gently, deeply and energetically. I had an excellent osteopath. She was able to help me up to the P.P. Then I noticed that we are making diametrically opposed observations. She concentrates exclusively on the physical and physiological level and does not include the transformation through the Light within my body. She is not able to let the process be and unfold in space and time and she does not understand that I am going through a huge spiritual, subtle and energetic event. The first and last of all her observations is limited to the physical body. She just cannot put up with the fact that I am losing body mass. "How can you do that to yourself?" she moans with a mixture of worry and helplessness. It is obvious that through the bias of her medical background she is unable to summon up an understanding for subtle changes. Her formatting remains dominant and of prime importance, and she doesn't even register the transformations in my aura and in my prana body, in spite of her practicing kinesiology and partly using energy wo along with osteopathy. I observe, how our dialogue is more and more developing into two different monologues; we are talking about two different things. What disturbs me most are her fears. Not even the ones based on therapeutic diagnosis, but rather her fears of something new, of radical changes and metamorphosis, ... and about my weight-loss. No, what is for me most invasive are the negative thoughts which are indeed weakening me during the treatment. My frequency is reduced. I see and I feel that she is afraid, I perceive her doubts as well as her fears to be at the mercy of some unconscious remembrance from previous incarnations, when she herself was starved to death. As I am rather receptive, especially during a treatment, the effect of it is disadvantageous for me. Here, I should mention that my system together with my therapeutic clairvoyance nearly automatically switches over to observations and deeper perceptions. Right now, as I am lying on the therapy-couch, I find it difficult to switch off this ability voluntarily, also because of the widespread human and animal reflex of not having enough and particularly not having enough to eat also finds a resonance within me.

On the one side the osteopath does not know the P.P., which of course cannot be expected, on the other side there is no readiness on her part to include the perception of the subtle planes in her work. Of course, again, she has a right to that. Not only do I perceive a lack of understanding, but also a whole series of disadvantageous emotions and attitudes, among others the inability to accompany a process in a really holistic manner. Changes are categorized as pathological and not recognized as energetic, structural and as a temporary reaction of the system which is going through an intensive transformation. After the treatment I find the information of „lacking, not having enough" in my cells. Indeed, I can read the fears of my therapist in my cellular system. I am not only missing her support; her unconscious projections are disturbing me. Then I decide to end the therapy. So now, I let the Light do its job.

e) Support and assistance

At this stage I wish to emphasize how important it is to exclusively address real pranics or at least ex-pranic people, preferably the ones who are able to value individuality. The Light nourishment people, who have gathered first-hand experience and possess a medical or therapeutic background, are particularly recommended. Nobody else is appropriate, except for beginners attempting to do the P.P. who are not able to recognize their own needs and tend to over- or underestimate the reactions of their body. They indeed do require medical help.

Whoever has only read about pranic nourishment and whoever has set up analysis, theories and explanations is not a pranic person. Somebody whose partner has done the P.P. or still lives pranic, is himself / herself not a pranic person for he / she does not know the pranic state directly. The same applies to people who have gathered experiences with fasting, for they have not dealt with prana and light nourishment. It can be helpful to compare and draw similarities for the mind, the right side of the brain hemispheres, but one may not throw everything into the same bag. Scientific measures are useful, but they limit themselves to the physical, material body and display no other possibility to grasp the Light. At best Prof. Dr. Fritz Popp could measure the light within the cells of the pranic person with the special devices he has built to measure the light-content in the yellow of eggs. And this is only a supposition on my part. All other measurements do not really point to the main issue and are therefore worthless. And whoever has read or knows reports coming from the esoteric or the natural sciences might be an interested, well-read person, but he/she does not own a first-hand experience of prana. And in the worst case he/she is repeating something in a parrot-like fashion.

7. MY MEASUREMENTS

Apart from the capacity to observe things, which I developed as a nurse, I also have a fine perception, a trained intuition and an experienced sensitivity. The objective consideration of one's own processes is often threatened to be distorted or tainted by one's own fears or wishes.

This is why I make use of various charts and documents which provide me with objective results for my clients as well as for myself. I am fluent in the use of the pendulum and the dowsing-rod, which I teach, and I am in a position to verify my results through repetition and comparing with previous tests and follow up the evolution, and the changes taking place along the evaluations of the various measurements. There must be a comprehensible logic behind it, which corresponds to my observations and my subjective states, so that it makes sense. For example, when I feel exhausted, the vitality cannot be very high in the long run, etc.

If I deal with the vital index, I can first identify the general? life force but also the state of each organ and then measure radiasthetically its blockades and malfunctions in percentage. This also applies to the subtle bodies, the aura, and the chakras. All together this detailed information provides me with essential indications, which exhibit a reliable overview of the state of my health. Besides, I inquire about the state of the resistance and the immunity as well as the presence of the divine Light within the cell respectively through Aleph and Shin. To find out the appropriate harmonizing methods I make use of the scale of compatibility which gives precise results. Moreover, there is the possibility to try various experiments and tests and conduct empirical attempts. In other words, as a pioneer it is all about having the courage and the responsibility to gather observations and experience. My life is a series of experiments. Time and time again, I feel myself driven by a recurring curiosity to discover something new and better, which I test on my own body beyond the usual rules and paradigms. Adventure in the spiritual domain! In the end it has to be practical and realistic. It has to be helpful and suitable for everyday usage. And it has to improve and elevate daily life, human dignity and individual accomplishment.

Out of this perspective the measurements provide me with clear feedbacks. Besides, they represent a safety limit during P.P., which in turn gives me a reliable orientation, like a light in the tunnel which confidently guides my decisions. It is worth time and time again to make a "reality check". It may even prevent one from getting sucked in and boycotted by the general consensus with its so-called "reason" and "reasonable ways".

This task is not always easy. It demands a lot of clarity, objectivity and discrimination. The main danger lies in the fact that some personality aspects are still stuck in old thinking patterns like prejudices and fears (of the unknown, of being different, of the too much or too little), ignorance and lack of freedom pertaining to professional formatting with the dogmatic formulas "that´s how it should be", "that is not possible", "one may not", and all sentences starting with "one".

Beyond the limiting mind patterns, I would like to mention the "new religion", the so-called science. It measures, proves and verifies everything – just to refute it a few years later and replace it with the next truth – which is equally sustained by the new dogma. Everybody who can read has access to it and can understand what he wants to understand. One theory for everybody. But there is this exclusive monopole following the motto: This is how it is! It also applies to spiritual, esoteric, therapeutic and intellectual models. I know myself quite a few, I enjoy playing with them. I am even enthusiastic about some of them. I know what I am talking about, this is why I am allowing myself this satire. Yes, it is precisely my task to consider all these mental and emotional distractions and to eliminate them one after another with all their associations.

Then it is all about reducing the whole matter to its essence.

8. REACTIONS FROM PEOPLE AROUND ME

I had read about the possible reactions of family, friends and acquaintances.

I myself remember food scarcity and even starving in other lives. This is a world-wide topic of humanity (also in the animal world), everywhere in the world and in all epochs except at the present time in the West, where there has been such a proliferation of foodstuff only in the last 50 years, which is, however, not available to everybody. The fear of getting hungry, of not having enough to eat sits deeply engraved into the cells. One just needs to observe the behavior of customers, when supermarkets are closed for two days in a row, or if scarcity of any foodstuff is being announced, how people buy everything off down to the empty shelves and hoard even more than they can consume themselves. Hunger is an existential lack that pokes at our survival instincts. A well-fed inhabitant of the western world like me should not easily be endangered. So where do these fears come from?

Indeed, we all have one or possibly more past lives, in which we starved during wars, due to insufficient crops, being imprisoned and underfed – or even in this incarnation, when we repeatedly had to wait for the bottle as a baby. This is a program that quickly switches on "urgent" or "emergency".

In a more widespread sense, it triggers off the pattern of generally not having enough: not enough love, attention, possession, sex etc.

Minimal thinking, limiting beliefs and emotions are expressions of these patterns which generate corresponding actions and attitudes. We have two components here. On the one side fear and scarcity. Both are used to set people against each other since the beginning of humanity and also internalized as a pressure onto oneself. On the other side, there is greediness. Well, somewhere there is an overflow to which not everybody has access. "The haves and the have-nots" as the English say.

What about playing a different game someday, choose other paradigms and let humanity grow out of its infantile shoes? Let us decide, that each one receives whatever she/he requires, not more, not less! And that it is available directly from the source, because we live in alignment with it. This is indeed what gradually takes place when the accordance with the Light is being reached for.

So now we have gained a little insight and background into possible spontaneous reactions to the news "I am feeding on Light". On the whole, the manners of expression and behavior reflect the general tendency to meddle or interfere, to give advice in spite of not knowing and having no experience in the matter. Everyone thinks he/she has to give his / her "like "or "dislike" without being asked about his / her opinion. Superficial, ignorant and without experience. And most of all not wished or asked for.

A friend of mine asked pertinent questions about how I actually do this, another one has drawn interesting parallels to her fasting experiences as well as the feedback from her family. Two women asked me about my motivations. One and only one asked me how I am feeling. As I answered well, very well, she said "Good, then I am happy for you". My African friend, himself a highly spiritual person who is acquainted with ritual fasting, said to my P.P." Then you will not get ill", which I found a particularly interesting comment. There are ignorant remarks about the fear of deficiency symptoms, that also used to be addressed to vegetarians years ago. Nowadays hardly anybody dares mentioning them. Some comments may also come from so-called spiritual persons. It can even sound very schoolmasterly, when they quote their "masters", claiming that earth spirits and light beings do not agree to pranic nourishment. There are also critics who know what is meant by The Light, but who nevertheless claim that humans are not so far-advanced yet as to feed on Light. These claims originate both from occidental as well as oriental persons. Holy books do mention the Light, but for human beings there is only sweat, work, sin, suffering – and a great deal of it – painful birthing, eternal and insatiable yearning for the Light ... staying small, suffering, incomplete, not knowing. Maybe sometime, on the other side, there will be Light...But not now!

I also have colleagues and therapists who whisper in my ear as they are parting:" Be careful!" I usually answer: "What about, then?" How much have you lost till now? Will you lose more weight? The air does not contain calories. How much do you weigh now? These are the questions of the "weight specialists", who ascertain with their critical eye that I have lost weight, that I am even thinner than last time and that there will soon be nothing left of me.

I try and explain that I am doing a change-over in my diet now, absorbing pure energy, that I am not on an emaciating diet. But they only see the (missing) mass. Their fear makes them project exaggerated images upon me. They do not register that I have a different radiance, that I exude health and vitality and that in spite of weight-loss the tone of my skin is relatively taut and fresh (for my age). They do not see that I now live in my proper body again and that I am not so thin anyway, for I have a strong musculature.

Then there are people who are stubbornly convinced right from the beginning that there is no such thing as pranic nourishment and that it is not possible anyway. It just does not fit into their narrow, pitiful world. They do not know anything about the P.P., do not need to discover the international tradition of pranism or to hear, how a modern and scientific person deals with it. They have made up their mind, it has all been already decided: It does not work, not possible. Such an attitude in the City of Munich in the 21st century seems inconceivable to me. Obviously, I should widen my horizon myself: Indeed, it is possible to be stubborn and ignorant and to want to remain that way.

On the other hand, for the doubters the pranic person eats secretly or they simply accuse her/him of lying. But they do believe everything the politicians tell them. Funny, isn´t it?

And some spiritual persons who are themselves working with the Light think the conversion to Light nourishment is not realizable.

Now and then someone advises me that I definitely should take proteins, maybe also iron. Such recommendations depend upon the interest, the knowledge and the experience or the priorities of the persons sharing them. In the realms of pranic nourishment the human being is not considered to consist of a collection of chemical substances, where one or the other ingredient is constantly missing.

And then there is the family, who is basically and mainly worried about me and is just afraid. A real plague for the pranic person. Worry, apprehensions, imagined scenarios with catastrophic, irreparable consequences are not expressions of love, but, on the contrary, negative projections which paralyse both sides and rob them of their strength. They surround the recipient with murky clouds of neurotic, weakening energy. Groundless fears or vague worries based on assumptions and not on information lower the frequency, I repeat, of both sides: the ones who worry and the ones whom the worries are intended for. It is of the utmost importance, that this mechanism should be understood, for it does not only occur in the personal domain, but on a wider scale such as in the family, in business, in society, national and planetary. We spoil each other's future prospects and developments through gloomy pictures about the world and life in general, through nagging fears and latent uncertainties. For ourselves, our private encounters, our collectivity, for the whole of humanity.

Stop talking nonsense, just repeating what you've heard without reflecting, open your eyes (instead of sticking your head in the sand or hoping that somebody else will bring a solution) and start clearing up your own mess! Then you will attract and meet other courageous people, who also pull up their sleeves in order to entirely change the status quo down to the basement. All according to individual capacities and possibilities. Each one of us in her/his own manner. It is better than sitting in front of the TV half hypnotized and getting worried, isn't it? That is the reason why you are incarnated: to participate in the big RE-NEW-ALL. (One of Vicky Wall's expressions. She brought Aura Soma into the world and played an important role in my spiritual development.)

One more word concerning fear: Fear is the only emotion that keeps the Light away and reduces the intake of Light.

Moreover, this constellation of being afraid (worry - nagging concerns) functions like a pressure lever: You're doing something different from us all. This is dangerous. That's why I am worrying. You do not want me to feel unwell and be concerned about your welfare, do you? Here is my answer: Take responsibility for your emotions, instead of dumping them onto me, for you will receive no pity from me.

It is so much more enriching to be supportive at the right time, to be loving and respectful, helpful, present and active.

Preferably, when you are expressedly called for or requested to offer your assistance. In a certain way the person knows what she / he is doing, she / he is being led by her / his higher wisdom, her / his inner guidance, her / his common sense, by her / his insights and intelligence. Practice trust and respect the free will of the person in front of you. You can strengthen her /him with light, love and confidence and express your caring by enveloping her/him in Light, affection and trust. This raises your vibration as well as hers. And the frequency of the whole world. If you encounter something that you do not know or cannot understand, you can get yourself the necessary information and you can ask questions. Or do you prefer giving the impression that you know everything and still talk rubbish? As a matter of fact, this looks rather silly and ignorant. Please spare yourself and others any unasked-for opinions and unwished for advice, any know-it-all attitudes and gullible comments.

I treat this topic very thoroughly, because these encroaching attitudes do not only concern pranic people and Light nourishment. To interfere with other people's affairs with the intent of changing them seems so widespread that this can even lead to wars. There is always one who is convinced to know what is right for everybody and that she / he has to impose it upon everybody else. Of course, always with the best intentions of the world!

And now I shall include the systemic model, especially as it pertains to the family, but it is also applicable to all systemic constellations. In this realm family is considered to be a living organism where each member assumes a role, that aims at reaching a balance for the whole. Seen from this angle, my enthusiasm and eagerness to experiment are being balanced with concern and worry. As I do not feel myself as a victim within a system, but rather as a self-responsible individual, I straightaway brush off the damping effects of this approach by not even wasting my time with it. However, I prefer sharing my experience with people in an interesting and enriching exchange.

Let us share the best we have with other human beings and with the world! Let us accept the others as being different and let them wear what they want and not wear what they do not want to wear, let us let them love each other as they like and honor the God or the force which fulfills them. This is the way Life is meant to be: an endless abundance of multiple expressions of the one Light. Aliveness, the Life, is the opposite of the clone or the remote-controlled robot or the stubborn, uniform dogma in narrow minds.

During the process, as I was losing weight, I sometimes heard two entirely contrary opinions within ten minutes. Either: "Oh dear, one can´t see you any more, you´re so thin!" or: "You look so good, younger and lighter. So full of Light!" Who is right? Who is projecting what? I let you know a secret: I am a magician. Sometimes I look this way and sometimes the other. That is what is called form-shaping. I let you decide which version is the right one!

After having integrated the pranic nourishment already for several months, I am sometimes asked, whether I shall soon stop the process or how long I still want to stay without food. Then I explain that the installation of prana takes place during the 21- day process. I have now been living in the pranic modus for X months. The person asking may become speechless and look at me in surprise or in a light shock and say: "Well, you´re still alive and you look good." What is happening there? First of all, the old thinking says: No, you cannot live, work, travel, go hiking in the mountains without eating. Impossible. Then the person asking opens her eyes, looks at me now. The overcome belief is being revised through present observation: Yes, she is alive, and she looks healthy. This new understanding means: It is indeed possible. It will get registered in the spectrum of human possibilities and therefore widen the general awareness of humanity.

I also wish to mention the few people who have express no comment referring to my physical changes or my new mode of nourishing myself. Some are uncertain, others do not have any interest in this topic, know nothing about it and regard the process as my personal decision. Nevertheless, they are not completely indifferent. One of them said, she would read my book. As she does not know anything about pranism she does not say anything about it. A respectable and wise attitude.

Now, last but not least, and a secret between you and me: Feeding on Light has to do with different paradigms, not even new ones, for pranism is definitely nothing new and no fashion either. It corresponds to a basic transformation of consciousness, which expresses itself through Life down into the cells and in the daily behavior.

Now let us have a look at the effect and mechanisms of the reactions on the pranic persons and how they function.

9. TRANSFORMING NEGATIVE PROJECTIONS

In the context of my conversion to Light nourishment I define certain mental and emotion expressions as negative as far as they reduce or interfere with my vibrational rate. Their source is either external or internal, that is foreign in origin or self-owned, sometimes though a mixture of both, for ex. in the case of internalized family or societal believes.

What is decisive for me is the manner in which I deal with blockades, "brakes" and similar occurrence and in the end what I make out of them. It is most important to have knowledge and insights about oneself, especially what is pertaining to extreme tendencies.

Occasionally doubts and oscillations may offer the possibility to consider the project from another perspective, to weigh pros and contras, to question and to revise aspects of the personality and to draw new conclusions. I hardly take seriously the rare doubts and fluctuations which crop up during the P.P. I observe them at a distance and do not let myself be overwhelmed by them. On the contrary, I turn them around and make out of their negative influence a source of inspiration and strength.

After asking myself how far this message is valid, I decide whether I switch it off or whether I use it as a confirmation for my experiment.

A very sound power of decision is of course a prerequisite and it will leave little space for doubts. The latter do lead people into conflicts. Torn apart and hesitant, they hardly come along on their way and know not who they are. On planet earth polarity reigns: everything has two sides and it is clever and intelligent to weigh them out. Weakened and inhibited by doubts, it is easy to fall into the dichotomy and to be the prey of inner arguments, instead of developing one's authentic strength in one's own life and in the world. Otherwise it is like driving with the brakes on, wishing and hoping and making compromises all the way through. Instead of knowing one's path and treading it.

Doubts are the one side, fear the other side of the negative medal. The animal, personal, unconscious, collective and cultivated fears belong to it. They are all part of a wide spectrum of brain washing together with old programs like starvation, food rationing and other limitations and contingencies, which are constantly making things look rare or unreachable. There is a fight for everything: living space, jobs, foodstuff, air, water etc.

It is an old trick that still and ever functions to set up the earth inhabitants against each other. Another old trick is that some want to grab the whole thing to themselves. And the others play the game although they are the majority. To opt out of the dilemma is the least one can do.

Unconscious fears are probably in the background of my constant weight loss. I have done some research the beliefs and programs behind them. In my cells I find some of the misery and hunger my mother suffered from during the war. She sometimes told me about it. She put a lot of pressure on me to eat everything up and more than I needed etc. Energetically I can scan her fears being carried over from beyond through to my sisters, it means, there exists a strong resonance within my sisters that is unconsciously receptive for this pattern that they tend to exhibit towards my experiment.

A couple of months after the end of the P.P., I decided to give up the topic "loss of weight", as long as I feel well. As a matter of fact, it is all about finding my rhythm and following it. With this decision I disconnected myself from other people´s pity and their exaggerated and energy zapping lamentations. These so-called good intentions carry and project a nagging weakening influence in the auric field of the pranic person. Basically worries, concerns and all fears diminish the vibrational rate and the life force on both sides. They surround the person with a light unclear cloud that is porous and slightly trembling. And to the effect of negative thoughts and emotions on the cells: a heavy frequency wraps up the edge of the cell with a dark boarder. Fearful thoughts leave grey clouds in the aura which may be very permeable during the P.P. Mental, psychic and energetic distortions hurt and cause pain deep into the soul.

Finally, I use them all as burning material for I dispose of a special mechanism: the more pressure there is to deter me from my plan, the more decisive and tougher I get. This is how I have functioned for the last 60 years. So you can imagine I have had lots of praxis.

And here I wish to thank all people near and far from the bottom of my heart, who have accompanied me in a positive manner. From the ones who, have no interest in the pranic process but trust me nevertheless to those who make the effort to understand the process and lend me their intelligent and respectful support. All my gratefulness goes in particular to Karin for her valuable and very active assistance.

The cloud of worries uses up a lot of strength and robs courage, decision power and will. It renders the path more difficult and inhibits through doubts and emptiness. On the opposite confidence, optimism, élan and drive provide you with security self-assertion. To trust somebody means that we take him seriously and are confident in his positive qualities, capacities and actions in the knowing that his intent leads him to successful results and fulfill his needs. Of course, it also applies to her! The fact of trusting a priori and in advance actually helps the person to connect more easily to her Higher Self, to make use of her discrimination and practice self-responsibility. How do you feel when one holds you for unable and unreliable? Just imagine, you are feeling particularly telepathic and permeable and thoughts as well as feelings from your acquaintances are penetrating your aura and your body like painful spears and other projectiles. Thought forms together with their corresponding feeling possess form, frequency, color and motion. Their effect and their vibration are similar to their meaning. So please visualize now that your aura is very open, that you are unusually receptive, permeable and telepathic. You are finding yourself in a metamorphosis, where old rules are not valid anymore and where you are still trying new ones out. You perceive that the people around you do not trust you, do not understand you and that they meet you with a fearful and uncertain look. Of course, not all of them, but people who are close to you and who mean a lot to you. It is painful. Sure, you can ignore them and with time you will only communicate with a few. I know a few pranics who ended up isolating themselves to avoid silly talks and remarks. There is a golden rule: never waste time with the people who know it all although they have no idea and no experience with breatharianism but still want to argue and discuss about it. There is nobody to convince. Nothing to prove. They are right. Stop. There is a particular spiritual path to follow namely yours. In your own individual manner. And you are taking responsibility for it-to 100 per cent.

Another objective of this discourse about heavy thoughts and emotions is to focus the awareness on the effects of human mental and emotional energy on their surroundings. This is namely a major cause of pollution. The neglect or even the distorted use which is made of the mental human dimension is alarming. I wonder where the intelligence of modern man has gone lost. Overloaded by superficial gossips, non-logical conclusions, collective beliefs which have grown on undifferentiated old drummed in knowledge, that have developed into overhauled thought patterns that are caught in automatism, reactions (instead of actions) and born of formatted fear scenarios through which he has lost the sight of his greatness. No, this is not a supplementary problem. This is the sole and only one.

10. WHAT IS LIGHT-NOURISHMENT?

This is lightful nourishment and nourishing Light out of the Light, that keeps us alive in eternity as part of the endless Light of which we are all made which is contained in All That Is.

There is an invisible and a visible world. The latter is generated by the first one. The material world bathes in a cosmic ocean out of ether and Light. Already a few decades ago Max plank, Albert Einstein and the new physics have defined and described the quanta as well as the light emanation and the light quanta. But we still think like in the 18th century: we believe there is only air between the objects. It is comparable to somebody claiming that the earth is flat. Still hasn´t caught up on the last discoveries. I do not have much knowledge about physics but I can perceive the Light of metaphysics.

Let us start with a couple of simple tips about physics.

The ether with its two components (aither and either) is the sustaining medium for the expansion of light in cosmos which permeates the whole of space. Together with Light it is the basic, fundamental substance from which everything emanates. Even Einstein hat revised his view of things somewhere along his carrier and he rehabilitated the ether, which was recognized and named as such in antique Greece.

It builds the basic stuff, the soul of the world, the common element of all life. It is in constant movement and flow, whirls, pulsates and rotates.

Scientifically light has been identified as visible and invisible light within the color spectrum and the wavelength realms from cosmic high rates down to extreme frequencies. The range goes from extreme high UV rays of 10 (high 24) Hz down to extremely fine infrared (0,1 up to 30Hz) and covers a huge variation out of which a very small amount of rays and colors are perceived by human beings.

Pr. Dr. Fritz-Albert Popp had special devices build to measure the light. Through this research he lost his professor title for a while, because one does think like in the 18th century or earlier only on the street but also in normal laboratories.

Researchers in Japan and in Russia have also been examining and studying bioplasma, biophotones and the Light within the cells for decades. Even much earlier the baron of Reichenbach described what he called Od which can be perceived by clairvoyants. Wilhelm Reich made revolutionary experiments with the life force and which he named first heliod then later orgon.

I remember meeting a student of the work of Carl Huter (famous German physiognomist) on the street of Zürich who said to me: "Oh you have a lot of helioda!" He was gone before I could ask him what he meant by helioda. After this encounter I started looking for the Light within as well as in books and through study.

The Kirlian method measures the force of the light rays together with the state of the life force and helps people to recover a healthy balance.

The inner aspects of light are mentioned in metaphysic and religious literature. This is the light of the world, lumen in Latin, the essence, the non-material aspect of consciousness and of individual awareness, that is connected with the inner Light source and the development of the personality. The thought processes and the thought forms exercise a telepathic influence upon the bioplasma. The power of thought impregnates the water in the glass but also the fluids within the physical body. On the other hand, there are Light waters which are located at various sources in the world (often related to Marian apparitions) and at power places, as researched by Dr Enza Ciccolo who developed a healing system based on the different water qualities.

Light water is nourishment. It contains all frequencies which are also present in sun rays. It is easy to make sun water and moon water. I have also charged sun globules after Jacob Lorber for a while. So now I am going back to the mystical concepts of light.

And I think of the light in Sufism and of Mazda, the Light bringer as opposed to darkness in Zoroatrism.

The Light contains endless aspects, but it is in itself a unity. This is why we are part of the unity and basically one with the Whole and with each other: we are all sisters and brothers.

Parallel to my pragmatic experience with pranism I am also interested in the theoretical explanations and include the observation of the energetic and subtle aspects during the metamorphosis of the chakras and the aura. Nevertheless, I have no dogmatic conclusions. It would be out of place to generalize my personal considerations for I came to the conclusion that there are various pranic states and that prana nourishment cannot be reduced to measuring, opening and closing chakras, to activate the pituitary and epiphysis glands or to influence or manipulate in whatever manner. There is no exact timetable or recipe that can be used and followed by everybody. There is actually a similar misunderstanding with homeopathy in the hands of people who think allopathically: one remedy for this, one remedy for that. This way of thinking limits the vision and reduces the entire homeopathic concept and system the reduced to a schematic polarized model. This is a misconception of homeopathy which really aims to treat the person individually and in her entirety.

It is all about pure Light and pure Love, the essence of creation, the Light spark, that live within everything that is alive as life force. The quanta research has been able to prove many things and science increasingly confirms the age-old knowledge of mystics.

Everything that lives is made of Light that informs the various structures consequently also the human bodies. The Russian doctor and biophysician Alexander Gurwitsch has already discovered the informative interaction within the cells in the 20´s of the previous century. Ultra-dim cellular luminescence can be verified in the tissues of plants, animals and humans. The discoveries of Prof. Dr. Popp confirmed that biophotons are light quanta with ultra-dim light emanation. The Light within the cells pulsates in constant rhythms until the moment of death when it extinguishes and the ether body disintegrates as described by Jacob Lorber, the big Austrian mystic. When the person is alive it can also be perceived as the first fine emanation that radiates out of the body of vital people and sometimes named "health aura".

I could claim from now on that I am feeding on biophotons. It would sound much more scientific and not quite as exotic as prana. I wish to complete this text with the knowledge of Dr Diethard Stelzl. He reports that the epiphysis contains color receptors and a lentil through which the light rays are conducted to the cells. For him prana has the same meaning as life force.

What am I really feeding on? On everything and more, all out of the one unique stuff that there is, namely the Light, that expresses itself through numerous and endless variations and that make vividness to life. This actually is consciousness. And I nourish myself on it also when the sun is not shining. The access to the Light occurs through the chakras but also through beauty, goodness, love, harmony, joy, through exercises with phosphenes but also through intellectual work and physical movement. But mainly through the orientation of consciousness.

Why such a long text about the Light? Because most people have no idea and also no concept about the Light. This is the reason why most get scared when I say: I now live from Light or I am feeding on Light. They imagine me swallowing air or even Light. The results are misleading.

The Light contains everything. Everything that humans and all other beings require. Each person takes in or dare I say "ingests" Light with his food. This is scientifically measurable. Naturally biodynamic, live and raw aliments contain more light than refined foodstuff. This is the light that keeps living beings alive, not the calories, claim the researchers.

I also use Light in the sense of prana where pranism and pranics are derived from.

Here is a little exercise for you: if you like to experience prana in a visible manner, you can see the light particles on a sunny day by adjusting your sight looking beyond the objects. Soon the little transparent spheres appear and keep moving in the air full of life. This is part o the energy that generates and boosts life in all that is alive. Nothing strange, esoteric or frightening. Nevertheless, it looks as if modern man is afraid of it.

You can also activate the Light within through watching phosphenes. The word phosphen comes from the Greek "phos" for Light and "phainein" which means "to show or appear". They are defined as inner Light appearances which clairvoyant people perceive. They can be produced by shortly staring at a source of Light and closing the eyes immediately afterwards. These inner lights activate the epiphysis.

And we possess still another Light organ, namely the spleen which was considered for a long time as superfluous and useless. This society really has no idea about the Light!! The spleen remains an enigmatic and mystical organ. This is no wonder that William Leadbeater included it into the chakra system for it serves as indicator for the will to live, the joy of living, for drive and vitality. It may not be overlooked when testing the subtle system. When it is underactive, depression and lethargy as well as heart rates disturbances are detectable.

The Light content of foodstuff can be measured in Bovis units. This system of measurement was introduced by the engineer Alfred Bovis as a relative gauging index, an abstract, arbitrary scale to ascertain the intensity of Light energies and the degree of the life force. The Bovis units represent an appreciable scale index among radiesthesists. All beings whether human, animal or plants feed on Light. The Bovis units of natural honey reach up to 11000 BU and contain 100% Light. It means honey van be an adequate source of light for pranic people who occasionally need extra nourishment for ex. by weight loss, weakness or pronounced sensibility to cold temperatures. It nearly produces no excrement, hardly influences the sleep duration and only consumes a small amount of digestive energy.

At this point it should be understandable that the P.P. is actually a change over from material to subtle nourishment or diet, comparable to the conversion from a carnivorous diet to one without meat or from a vegetarian diet to a vegan one or even from a usual way of consuming bread and noodles to a gluten free diet. The conclusion is that the pranic person still feeds on something, namely Light. As opposed to a person who goes without material nourishment without replacing by whatsoever as it is the case by anorexia or in hunger strike.

Have you succeeded in solving the question: "What is the difference between pranic nutrition or feeding on Light and fasting? At the beginning I found it difficult to make out the difference between them, because at first sight they show parallels. That is one reason why it is recommended to gather experience with short and longer fasting periods before starting the P.P., so as to get acquainted with some of the body experiences various reactions during the change-over. Each person is different, and each body is variably burdened with toxins. This means that the ways in which the body is eliminating these toxins and to what amount are completely individual. Also, the personal tolerance level in dealing with reactions and discomfort varies from one person to another.

People who have been fasting also know that no fasting period is identical to the previous one. Nevertheless, knowledge and experience contribute to the ability to discriminate and to anticipate the incoming reactions: You know what is normal in this context and what is not. Although both processes show similarities, there is an essential difference between fasting and breatharianism. In the first process I am renouncing solid food without replacing it. That means I am living on the resources of the body. During the P.P. material nourishment is substituted by subtle nutrients. The connection to and the assimilation of prana is practiced. Or, considered from another point of view, the prana, the Light within the cells and the aura is activated, so as to establish a growing resonance with the endless Light source. In other words, you cannot fast forever, because the reserves of the body will run out at some point. The connection to Light, on the contrary, is inexhaustible, and therefore it is possible to definitely change over to the Light as a source of nutrition on all levels. Feeding on Light, as long as the PP is complete and thorough, that is as long as it provides a lasting and energetic metamorphosis, brings you closer to eternity and infinity.

And I have to say no to the lady Dr of chemistry who asked me whether I have to sit under the lamp to feed on Light. With Light we mean in this context the Light of the world, the eternal and endless Light of the Soul which we absorb through the subtle anatomy of the aura layers especially the prana body(but not only), through chakras and other energy centers, through the cells and the atoms of the physical body. Through the love, the power and the will of the cosmos, other humans and all other living beings whether visible or invisible with whom I share this life of mine. Through beauty and goodness and the radiance of this world and other dimensions with which I am connected. Exactly as you are doing it...only a little more coherently, more intensively and with more awareness.

11. THE EFFECTS OF PRANA

On the physical plane I have recovered the flexibility of my youth. Before the process I was already or still in a good state of health. Through prana nourishment my general health and vitality have even improved. Pain immunity which developed during the P.P. remained afterwards. This particularity is for me unexpected and surprising. As a young girl I was fascinated by reports of Cathars who were burnt at the stake and hardly showed signs of discomfort. I know of incarnations of mine as a Cathar. I assume a correlation between the higher level of Light in my cells and the reduction of the pain sensitivity. I should research this in depth. I dispose of more physical strength and a good resistance. I have already reported about the positive changes in the skin appearance and the sleep duration.

My senses are finer and more differentiated: they offer me a greater amount of nuances pertaining to the appreciation and the enjoyment of taste, smells, colors, sounds and grades of Light intensity. I have spoken of hedonism: my surroundings unfold as a source of sensual experiences, which make me all the more enthusiastic. The lust of life, the joy of harmonious colors, shapes, people, spaces, landscapes etc. fill me with delight and fulfill my mind.

The conversion to prana offers me a big liberation from the compulsion of daily life which I previously I had already reduced to a large degree. On the other hand, I have set myself a strict set of spiritual and professional as well as physical practices and rules. Nevertheless, I have chosen them freely and they are meaningful for me. I have become more precise, thorough and coherent. I hope not too pedantic. Astonishingly enough I am also much more practical and I can repair a few things where I used to have two useless hands. To be honest some of these methods are very unusual and tradesmen would burst into laughter at the sight of my work. But they function! I enjoy a better rapport to the material world. It seems to be participating and encouraging in co-creation whereas we use to lead power fights where I would necessarily be the frustrated loser.

I never have been particularly diplomatic, but this quality has not improved now. I do not intend to hurt people, but I want to call a cat a cat. I dispose of an increased mental clarity and precision, and I am able to categorize and to look through things especially motivations included my own. I can work in a more concentrated manner and with more perseverance.

The less I try and control things the better they unfold, and the pieces of the puzzle join together. The inner sight and the guidance build a strong intuition. I increasingly experience ecstatic moments independently from outside events.

12. PUBLIC RAMIFICATIONS OF PRANA NOURISHMENT

Those who have the task to bring pranism out to the public to contribute to the Whole and to stimulate progress have partly been rejected in their efforts and have sometimes been the object of animosity. Jasmuheen the famous and inexhaustible pioneer of Light nutrition who is travelling the world and working together with the United Nations advising on options to relieve starvation through pranism is an admirable woman. Of course, she has met at times with stupidity, narrow mindedness and ignorance. But she is made for this task and she sticks to her soul purpose. Right from the beginning I felt inspired by her but not convinced. Nevertheless, I am very grateful to her for her courage, her exemplary behavior, her generous thinking for she is considering breatharianism as a transforming chance for humanity at large.

The person who definitely convinced me is the German scientist and anthroposophist Dr Michael Werner, Doctor of chemistry and leader of the anthroposophical healing institute in CH-Arlesheim. In 2001 he achieved the 21-day P.P. under medical observation as he describes in his book. After which he remained pranic. In October 2004 after surmounting a few obstacles with the Swiss ethic commission he managed to have all scientific tests done under constant video observation and complete isolation for ten days at the University Clinic Lindenhof of Bern. The results of this spectacular study have only been published four years later. It simply mentions a "fasting" condition!!! In 2007 another study is being conducted in Prague with Michael Werner. The responsible leader of the study simply refused to publicize the results without providing any reason for his refusal.

This is what I call cowardice. Scientific cowardice. For these kinds of scientists, I do not have the least respect, for they are only busy with maintaining the status quo and confirming the general consensus and what everybody is supposed to believe in. Everything else gets suppressed, concealed and frowned upon. That remains me of Prof. Dr. Alexander Eben who has had an exceptional near-death experience and was also confronted by the narrow-mindedness and ignorance of other doctors and scientist. And there is Dr Rath and so many others known and unknown. What kind of fear motivates these people to hold on so tightly and stubbornly to the knowledge that has been drummed into their brains instead of widening up their horizon? Are they so formatted that they cannot think independently any more or are they afraid to lose their reputation, their titles and their money?

In front of such a distorted reality and as far as I am able to, I decide to sever the umbilical cord linking me to this pathological-not to say schizophrenic-consensus. From this point of view, I join the Afro American Genesis Sunfire who considers pranism as the only well aimed and consequent action to deter a system that lies and exploits without inhibition. Out of this perspective pranism could be defined as a peaceful and non-violent uprising. The last aspect which I shall not develop here, is the destructive and killing rage of humanity towards animals and nature which it cruelly disfigures and exploit to a large degree to feed itself.

To quote Stéphane Hessel: "To start something new means resisting. Resisting means starting something new"

13. CONCLUSION

The change over to pranic nourishment is one of the most important decisions of my life. It is a freely chosen Transformation. The longer it extends the better it gets: more stable and more balanced. I do not miss any of the daily rituals associated with food such as shopping, cooking, clearing up and neither eating outwards. My dedication to spirituality is more intense and I feel better connected to eternity and to infinity than ever.

My pranic experience is a series of vivid moments with insights and conclusions. I enjoy sharing them with interested people out of two reasons: first to anchor the breatharian metamorphic field, second to demystify this subject. I report my first unsuccessful endeavors, my detoxification and other down to earth experiences. I am an average woman with a maybe not so common story. This process is certainly not everybody's "cup of tea". I am aware of it and I do not encourage anybody to follow it. I would even definitely not recommend it to some persons and even advise against it. But for me now it is, and it feels coherent and enriching. My subjective perception of my condition has been helpful and has confirmed me in my unique approach to this pranic way.

I would like to end with a citation of Michael Werner: "It is not a matter of giving up eating, it is a matter of thinking differently". It is not about measuring, statistics or counting calories. Otherwise we are remaining on the level of fighting for particles. Eating or not eating, caught up in the contraries and polarity. However, there is the possibility to adopt another perspective similar to the triangle. From there one enters a higher dimension which transcends the never-ending loop, and which vibrates on the level of the waves. There the "as well as" is possible and the whole gains another value and meaning. One is not stuck on the material plane alone anymore, but rather in a space where subtlety and other paradigms are necessary.

At the moment I feel well in the pranic mode. I work and travel a great deal. I am grateful for my life. My intuition lets me know of a bigger transformation and tells me that breatharian living is for me only a springboard. So it goes on. Maybe I shall let you know how.

My present situation fulfills me, but I expect it to unfold and deepen and to remain an ever-evolving challenge. I exclusively follow my own intuition and Higher Instance. If for any reason I am not feeling well any more or if I receive the impulse that pranism is not the right thing for me anymore, I shall carefully and freely end this modus and switch to the next appropriate way of life. Otherwise I remain happy and pranic.

I TEACH MANY ENERGY AND SPIRITUAL SUBJECTS AS A GROUP, TO INDIVIDUALS AND AT A DISTANCE.

List of my present teachings

DECODING AND SOLVING INHERITED TRAUMA AND BLOCKS OF PREVIOUS LIVES

SUBTILE RADIONICS FORMATION

THE HOLISTIC VIEW DEATH PROCESS

THE WARRIOR POWER OF SYMBOLS AND SIGNS FOR HUMANS, ANIMALS, PLANTS AND SPACES

THE USE AND BENEFITS OF EAR CANDLES

ENERGY AND SPIRITUAL CARE FOR THE BACK

LEAD THE SOULS ATTACHED TO THE LAND DIMENSION TOWARDS LIGHT

AURATHERAPY TRAINING

The strength of hand healing

THE POWER OF CRYSTALS - ATLANTIC KNOWLEDGE FOR THE 21ST CENTURY

MAGNETISM AND TELEPATHY

THE ORACLE OF NATURAL STONES

THE ART OF BEING A THERAPIST

THE USE OF THE PENDULUM AND THE WAND IN THE PROFESSIONAL OFFICE

PERSONAL MESSAGES OF THE NEW YEAR

VISION BOARD - TURNING YOUR VISION INTO REALITY

For more information, you can reach me by SMS on 0049 (0) 175 94 21 791

A BIG THANK YOU TO ANDREAS LÜHRIG!

FOR HIS WONDERFUL SIMILIS CARDS which can be ordered at the following address: www.sein-erleben.de

THE AUTHOR

The author was born in 1953 in Paris. Since childhood she has had a subtle, strongly pronounced perception.

She is a state certified nurse, specializing in psychiatry.

She is active as a lecturer in the most renowned German naturopathic school - Paracelsus Schulen - in Switzerland and Bavaria.

She offers training in radionics, auratherapy etc. at European level as well as care and lessons. As a therapist, she works both in person and remotely, for example by telephone, in French, German and English.

She has a lot of training in radionics - Radionic Practitioner of the Radionic Association, as well as training with David Tansley - in auratherapy, aromatherapy, lithotherapy, radiasthesia etc. She completed Aura Soma chromotherapy training with Vicky Wall and she is one of the first Aura Soma trainers.

Contact:

Aurélienne Dauguet

Landline: 0049 89 51 81 85 51

Literary reference

Aurélienne Dauguet

Reiseführer zu deinen kosmischen Energien -

Aura Entdeckung

ISBN 978-3-944700-02-1 (Paperback)

ISBN 978-3-944700-12-0 (e-Book)

Aurélienne Dauguet

AURATHERAPIE

für ÄRZTE, THERAPEUTEN und interessierte LAIEN

ISBN 978-3-96051-055-0 (Paperback)

ISBN 978-3-96051-056-7 (Hardcover)

ISBN 978-3-96051-057-4 (e-Book)

Aurélienne Dauguet

Mein neues Leben mit der Lichtnahrung

ISBN 978-3-96240-554-0 (Paperback)

ISBN 978-3-96240-555-7 (Hardcover)

ISBN 978-3-96240-556-4 (e-Book)

Aurélienne Dauguet

NOURRITURE LUMINEUSE

MA NOUVELLE VIE AVEC LE PRANISME

ISBN: 978-3-944700-07-6 (Paperback)

ISBN: 978-3-944700-67-0 (e-book)

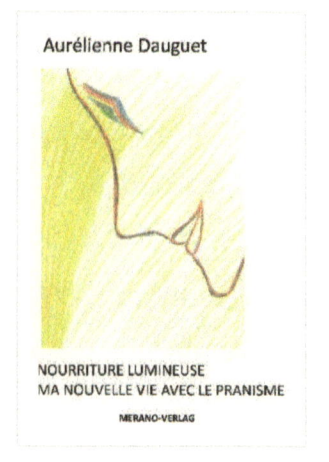